PRAISE FOR *JEWISH PRAYERS OF HOPE AND HEALING*

"Alden Solovy is a craftsman of words. I wish I'd had some of these prayers when I needed them most. I look forward to using Alden's thoughtful *tefilot* in my own *davening*."

—Rabbi David Levin-Kruss, Pardes Institute of Jewish Studies, Jerusalem

"A loving guide for people searching for a way forward."

—Rabbi Susan Silverman, author of *Casting Lots: How Raising My Children Helped Me Find God*

"Authentic, honest, and alive . . . With prayers for every season and circumstance, this book brings God into everyday life. It touched my heart deeply and awakened me to God's presence all around."

—Rev. Dr. Margaret Benefiel, adjunct faculty, Andover Newton Theological School; author of *Soul at Work* and *The Soul of a Leader*

"This beautiful book of prayers offers a masterful set of conversations with God. Alden's writing is elegant and inspiring."

—Rabbi William H. Lebeau, former vice chancellor for rabbinic development and immediate past dean of the Rabbinical School of the Jewish Theological Seminary, is senior consultant for rabbinic and institutional leadership for the Rabbinical Assembly.

"The honesty and simplicity of Alden's words reach just the place where the soul knows joy and sorrow and where God's spirit draws us to prayer. I count myself grateful and blessed that Alden's prayers from his faith tradition find a home in my own heart and in the hearts of my Christian readers."

—Pastor Austin Fleming, parish priest, Archdiocese of Boston; author of *Prayerbook for Engaged Couples*

"*Jewish Prayers of Hope and Healing* speaks from a place of deep spiritual connection to people of all faiths. It's a collection inspired by the ancient Jewish yearning for God that speaks to us all."

—Susan Diamond, founder and publisher, Prayables; contributing publisher/editor, Beliefnet

JEWISH
PRAYERS
of HOPE *and*
HEALING

JEWISH PRAYERS
of HOPE and HEALING

Alden Solovy

Kavanot Press

For information regarding permission to reprint material from this book, please e-mail your request to: info@kavanotpress.com.

Special discounts are available on quantity purchases by synagogues, churches, hospitals, hospices, other medical and religious organizations, associations, corporations and others. For details, contact the publisher at the e-mail address above.

Published by Kavanot Press, USA

Cover photograph © Martin Sykes-Haas

Martin Sykes-Haas is a Jerusalem-based photographer specializing in pictures of the Old City, street views, abstracts and large-scale decorative images. www.jerusalemphotographs.com

Cover and text design by Bookwrights.com

Manufactured in the United States of America

First Printing, 2013

Library of Congress Control Number: 2013915353

ISBN: 978-1-940353-15-9

IN MEMORY OF
Ami Diane Braziel-Solovy, *z"l*,
who always saw the writer in me,
even when I did not

IN HONOR OF
our daughters, Nikki and Dana,
a new generation of talent

CONTENTS

For Those Who Donated Their Bodies to
Medical Research   60
Meditation on the Burial of a Young Child . . .   61
At the Hand of Violence: A *Yizkor* Prayer . . .   62
After a Deadly Rampage   63
Yizkor for a Soldier   64
Yizkor for First Responders   65
Remembering 9/11   66
For 9/11 Survivors   66
At the Hand of Terror: A 9/11 *Yizkor* Prayer .   67
At the Hand of Terror II: A 9/11 Memorial
Prayer   68
Memorial Prayer for 9/11 First Responders . .   69
Holocaust and Anti-Semitism   70
At the Hand of Anti-Semitism: A *Yizkor* Prayer   70
Shoah Memorial Prayer   71
After the Horror   72
Tears of Crystal, Tears of Broken Glass   73
Munich Massacre Memorial Prayer   74

Healing the Body   77
General Prayers for Healing   78
Quick Prayer for Healing   78
Quick Prayer for My Healing   79
Quick Prayer for Healing (specific)   80
Inviting Healing   81
This Well of Pain   82
For Endurance   83
Relief from Chronic Pain   84
Relief of a Loved One's Chronic Pain   85
On Recurrent Pain   86
Surgery   87
Before My Surgery   87
Before a Loved One's Surgery   88
Before My Child's Surgery   89

PROLOGUE

מִן הַמֵּצַר קָרָאתִי קָּהּ, עָנָנִי בַמֶּרְחָב קָהּ.

From my narrowness I call to God;
from the expanse God answers me.

—Psalms 118:5

Oof. I thought. Me? Write a prologue to a book of Jewish prayers? On the surface, I seem like a decent choice. A rabbi. A writer. Engaged in Jewish life cycle as a mother, wife and spiritual guide. And I live in Alden's home city of Jerusalem. A transplant from the United States, just like him.

But I'm haunted by my own insecurities and confusions as I pray. Do I look to fellow worshipers like a person with the proper *kavanah*, intention, as I pray? Why isn't this second nature? Why am I thinking these thoughts instead of reaching for God? Who is God, anyway? What is God? Maybe we are just random creatures in an accidental evolution of life?

What page are we on?

"*Min hameitzar karati Yah, anani vamerchav Yah,*" says the psalm. "From my narrowness I call to God; from the expanse God answers me." That's my prayer experience—which sounds exalted—until I admit that it's because I am so trapped in my own spinning thoughts that it is literally true. I find myself in a narrow place of self-absorption.

All the more are we trapped in the narrow places of illness, death of a loved one, loss of a marriage. What do you do when you find yourself there, stuck, blocked to prayer, to anything outside yourself? Even the most fervent among us stand, from time to time, in those speechless moments.

Alden's poetry and prayer clearly and lovingly name that place and locate you in it and then gently lead you out—to the expanse. This book is a loving guide for people searching for a way forward.

—Rabbi Susan Silverman, author of *Casting Lots: How Raising My Children Helped Me Find God*, is a writer who lives with her family in Jerusalem.

FOREWORD

The great shofar is sounded,
and a still, small voice is heard.

—From the *U'ntaneh Tokef*, High Holy Day prayer

In September 1988, I participated in the funeral of Alden's father, Jack, *z"l*. In the sanctuary of my former pulpit at North Suburban Synagogue Beth El in Highland Park, Illinois, where I served as rabbi for 10 years, I offered words of eulogy to honor the memory of my friend and congregant, who had been so supportive to me and the Jewish community. When Alden and I recently reconnected, I was saddened to learn of the tragic loss of his wife, but was deeply moved to learn how the power of prayer has provided him with direction and strength.

Jack died in the Hebrew month of Elul, the month preceding Rosh Hashanah and Yom Kippur, during which Jews prepare for the intense days of prayer and introspection known as the "Days of Awe." After 25 years, Alden told me, he still recalls my words of tribute for his father: "As I think of Jack today, I remember the *U'ntaneh Tokef* prayer of the coming High Holy Days. It tells us, '*U'vshofar gadol yetaka, v'kol d'mamah dakah yeshama.* The great shofar is sounded, and a still, small voice is heard.' The author of the prayer was saying that in the aftermath of the strong, glorious sound of the shofar that awakens and energizes our senses by its dramatic presence, the still silence that follows is filled with palpable energy that we experience as if it were a new sound. And so it is today that we feel the strong sense of Jack's presence even in our silence . . ."

Thirteen years later—again in the month of Elul, on the morning of September 11, 2001—as vice chancellor and dean of the Rabbinical School of the Jewish Theological Seminary, I was asked to convene an assembly for students, faculty and staff to address our devastation, grief and anxiety in the aftermath of the collapse of the Twin Towers. As men and women of many different faiths, colors, ethnicities and national backgrounds, we began that morning in silence, trying to comprehend the traumatic, life-changing events that we had seen and heard on television as the towers fell. The events of that day defied logic or explanation. Any words of advice or counsel would be inadequate as a source of comfort. Still, we had to move beyond our silence, so we prayed together.

After our gathering, those who were unpracticed in the art of prayer, and even those without any religious beliefs, acknowledged that our prayer had given voice to their own inner feelings and that the experience of praying as a community had provided strength. In the hours after the attack, on that most awful day, men, women and children were filling houses of worship. In countless places across the country, prayer groups assembled even beyond the confines of sanctuaries. Some emerged spontaneously on street corners and in coffeehouses. It seemed natural and intuitive that prayer was needed as an antidote to the paralysis of inaction that threatened to overtake us.

Prayer clearly stands at the heart of every faith community, but it is not exclusively the possession of people of faith. While there is ample evidence that prayer is helpful as a response to tragedy, prayer also provides a needed outlet when we want to give expression to overwhelming feelings of gratitude for our blessings at times of joy. In faith communities, traditional prayers in hymnals and prayer books used at fixed times assist the worshiper in addressing God. At other times, individuals with and without formal religious affiliation articulate feelings of joy, adversity or vulnerability to God more spontaneously through personal thoughts and spoken prayers.

Through the words of the Torah, Jewish tradition provides keen insight into the role of prayer in the human experience. We read of Noah, who, after 150 days on the water, aware of the destruction of the world as he knew it, is filled with the need to give thanks for his life and the safety of his family as the floodwaters receded. He built an altar to offer a sacrifice, even though God had not commanded him to do so, because in moments when feelings overwhelm, the human being needs to pray. When pained by barrenness, our Matriarchs prayed for children. Later in the Torah, Moses petitioned God to heal his sister, Miriam, from her leprosy. David gave prayerful voice to triumph, despair and hope through the poetry of his Psalms.

Through this extraordinary book, Alden Solovy offers the gift of an inspired writer to help all of us find comfort and direction. This book clearly flows from Alden's caring soul, the special soul that I first observed in him as a sensitive young man. These prayers pour forth from him because, as he has come to know more fully the joys and sorrows of life, he came to his own recognition of the need for human prayer. This recognition, which led him to understand the power of prayer in acquiring a deeper understanding of the meaning and purpose of life, also led him to share his discovery and his words with others.

This book will help those accustomed to traditional worship find new meaning in familiar prayers. Many who read Alden's story and his masterful conversations with God will accept Alden's encouragement to create their own prayers as a way of intensifying the personal relationship that each person can claim with God. Those new prayers, yet to be written, will add to the songs, poetry and prose that make up the enormous corpus of literature that we call prayer.

No matter how experienced one might be in the art of praying, *Jewish Prayers of Hope and Healing* is a significant addition to that literature. Although he began this book as a response to the most damaging experiences of his life, Alden discovered for himself and for us that prayer is meant not only for extraordinary, urgent moments. Rather, the most important reward of prayer is to be found in regular worship, celebrating the everyday, more routinely wonderful moments that we are privileged to experience and to articulate with our unique human abilities. Thank you, Alden, for providing new inspirational ways of assuring greater access to God as we offer our prayers.

—Rabbi William H. Lebeau, former vice chancellor
for rabbinic development and immediate past dean
of the Rabbinical School of the Jewish Theological
Seminary, is senior consultant for rabbinic and
institutional leadership for the Rabbinical Assembly.

INTRODUCTION

"Mommy?"

That's how my then-25-year-old responded to the news of her mother's imminent death. My wife of 27 years was visiting a friend in Maine—1,000 miles from our suburban Chicago home—and fell down a set of unfinished wooden steps. She fell hard. The resulting traumatic brain injury was massive.

"Yes," I replied. "Mommy."

It's a call that no father should ever have to make, a call that no daughter should ever receive. I would make the call twice that day. I reached my daughter Nikki in Denver first.

"Mom is going to die today. We're going to fly across the country and try to get there before she goes." Then the warning: "Dear, there's almost no brain function left. She won't know in a conventional sense that we're there."

"But she'll know we're there. Right, Dad?" Nikki asked. "She'll know?"

"Yes," I answered, "she'll know." Perhaps I lied. Perhaps I told the truth. I'll never know. Either way, I spoke from my heart. To this day, I have no idea where that answer came from. Faith, perhaps. Faith that God would make sure that some kind of meaning, some kind of beauty, would emerge from these moments of pain and death. Faith that a daughter's good-bye would be heard.

One call down, one to go. My younger daughter lived in a transitional neighborhood in Chicago proper. A heavy sleeper not accustomed to picking up the phone at 5:30 AM, Dana was much harder to reach. As I dialed her again and again, my sister in Virginia worked the phones with the airlines to get Dana and me on a flight to Maine.

I threw some things together into a suitcase and headed to the airport, not knowing my departure time or if I'd connect with my younger daughter before our as-yet-unbooked flight. I called Ami's *z"l* elder sister, who, in turn, called the rest of Ami's family. I tried Dana again and again. When I arrived at O'Hare, I received a call from my sister. The flights were booked. I don't remember who called my mother and my other sister.

Sitting on the floor in Terminal One, my back against the windows, I continued to attempt to reach Dana. I worried about missing the flight. I worried about leaving without her. Finally, Dana picked up. There was no time to spare. "You've gotta get into a cab now and come to the airport. Right now," I said. Then I told her why. "I'm sorry to tell you this way. I'm sorry we don't have time to talk. You have to move. We'll talk on the plane."

She had less than an hour to dress, pack and get from the city to the airport in time for our flight. She made it. We were nearly the last ones on the plane, headed to reunite with Nikki in order to say good-bye to a woman who was, for all intents and purposes, already dead.

In the month before Ami died, my meditation practice had shifted dramatically. Until then, my practice had been to sit for 15 minutes in the morning after reading two inspirational texts. Then I'd pray, using some classic Jewish prayers, as well as some prayers I created "on the fly" each morning. The prayers were usually on the same theme: the health and well-being of others generally—family and friends, in particular. After prayer, I'd write a gratitude list, a personal affirmation and my intentions for the day, as well as any specific observations that came to mind about my feelings and experiences in the past day or so.

The basic structure of this practice remained constant, but the meditation itself took on a sort of depth and breadth I could not explain. I'd begin the practice and, without noticing the flow of time, I'd lose most awareness until I had a sense that my meditation was over. An hour or more passed with my mind completely quiet.

Several times during the month, I'd say to friends, "I'm so full. This is so different, so new. I don't understand why I am so full." It was amazing. I felt like a river of blessings overflowing its banks. And I wondered—rather casually, it now seems to me—if God was preparing me for something. I kept that particular thought to myself.

––––––––––––––––––––––

A week after Ami died, I was completely empty. Out of gas. Out of energy. Out of emotion. I was a blank, less-than-zero shadow of a man making the motions of life. I stopped meditating. I stopped praying. I stopped writing. I didn't see this as a theological or an existential statement. I simply needed to get up in the morning—force myself up, really—and take care of the business of life. And family. And death.

I wondered, "How does a man call his daughters to say, 'Your mom is going to die today'?" I did it. I did it twice. The simple fact is that I have no idea how to do it. I know that somewhere, today, this very moment, another father is giving his children the worst news of their lives. Somewhere else, a mother is doing the same thing. I am convinced that, like me, they will understand what they did but may never understand how they did it.

I wondered, "Will I ever write another prayer? Will I ever want to pray or meditate or write a gratitude list again?" The questions felt stupid. Of course not. Why the hell would I ever write another prayer?

The question, however, had its own answer, a different answer. My children. What else could I really do for them but pray? One morning, without my usual morning process, a prayer moved from my pen to the paper, a prayer "For Bereaved Children." With my own hand and my own heart—guided by a Power I did not understand—I found the words that I needed to recite on behalf of my girls. In that moment, my view of my life shifted. The gift that I would give the world, in the shadow of Ami's death, would be a new voice of prayer.

Dana and I got to the hospital hours after we had expected to arrive. We were delayed and then diverted by rain and ultimately forced to rent a car and drive an hour and a half in a torrent in order to get to the hospital that evening. It was Friday night, Shabbat, and we were not thinking about celebrating the Sabbath or whether we'd still be driving after sundown. It was a harrowing drive toward a moment we did not want and could not fully imagine.

Nikki had already been at the hospital for hours, without her father and sister, in the shadow of her mom's impending death. My sister-in-law arrived two hours later. The nurses summoned a tray of food and beverages for us from the hospital kitchen. None of us had eaten for most of the day. We kept vigil together until about 1 AM, when the nurse suggested that we get some rest at a hotel on the hospital campus that was reserved for families of patients.

According to the law in Maine, brain death must be declared twice, at least four hours apart by two different doctors. At about 4 AM, I got a call from the nurse that the first declaration was imminent. I dressed and called my daughters and sister-in-law Donna. I told them that they had some time to shower and gather themselves, but to return to Ami's room in the ICU soon.

During the morning, after the first declaration of brain death, we finalized the organ donation paperwork. We each got some private time with Ami. We also sang together and told stories. At some point, Nikki said out loud how much it was bothering her to see all the blood in Ami's flowing blond hair. An ICU nurse must have overheard because a few minutes later, a woman came back and washed Ami's hair. Ami had already been declared dead once, but this nurse came to care for her, anyway. The nurse dried Ami's hair and said, to no one in particular, that she really wished that she had a pick-comb to untangle Ami's hair. Nikki went to her purse and pulled out a pick. "I never use this thing," Nikki said, "but Mom used to say that you should always have a pick in your purse. You never know when you'll need it." So we witnessed a moment of unexplained "coincidence." And we witnessed a moment of kindness and beauty at the edge of death.

A bit later, a rabbi arrived—the hospital must have arranged it—and sat with us. We talked together about Ami and then she read a *vidui*, a deathbed confession, on Ami's behalf.

The morning passed, and finally, the nurse let me know that the time had come for the second declaration. "Time to say one last good-bye," I told the girls. Wordlessly, they walked together the few steps to the bed and then moved to either side of their mom. Each girl had a head on one of her mom's shoulders, and they held hands across her belly, eyes closed, gently crying. There were no words, no sounds. After a few minutes, I escorted Nikki, and Donna escorted Dana out of the room. Like that, it was over. That was the last time we saw her.

We walked down a corridor toward the hotel, in shock, until one of my girls said: "Mom was lucky she died here." And the other said: "We were lucky she died here."

It was Saturday, the 10th of Nissan on the Hebrew calendar, the 4th of April on the Gregorian calendar, and *Shabbat Hagadol* in the Jewish religious cycle. Ami was 53 years old.

In the four years since Ami's death, I've written more than 400 prayers, meditations, poems and songs. Prayers of healing. Prayers of rejoicing. Prayers of mourning. Prayers of celebration. They cover topics ranging from the changing seasons to the grief of children, from the joy of song to the hope of healing. Some sound like poems, others echo the Psalms, some take on the voice of the ancient prophet and others speak through the wisdom of the Spiritual Traveler. They all begin in that place inside our souls that yearns for connection to God. These blessings come from a profoundly Jewish heart; yet they resonate among all people of spiritual intent.

The response to my work has been truly amazing. I could not have predicted it when I launched my website three years ago. I launched the site after participating in the New Warrior Training Adventure with the Chicago community of the ManKind Project. In that training, I selected a mission for my life, which I continue to attempt to live, day by day. My mission: "As a man among men, I bring holiness into the world through prayer, adventure, joy and wonder." As I thought about that mission, simply writing prayers was not enough. I needed to take those prayers into the world. So I began posting them online.

My prayers have now been read in more than 140 nations. They've been published in prayer books and spiritual journals, online and in synagogue and church handouts. I've been asked to write prayers for public commemorations—such as Veteran's Day and the 10th anniversary of 9/11—and for private use, including a rabbi's retirement and another rabbi's congregational installation. A hospital-based rabbi working in pastoral care asked me to write a prayer to be used at the removal of a child's life support. Another rabbi asked me to write a prayer for removing a wedding band. A Jewish educator asked me to write a fertility treatment prayer. Many of these prayers appear in this volume. I've collaborated with musicians and with clergy. My prayers have been used in Catholic churches, evangelical Christian worship, Jewish Sunday schools, a Methodist parochial school and in synagogues throughout North America and the world. Selected prayers have been translated into Hebrew, French and Russian.

———————

Writing prayers deepens my ability to pray. It has become a focal point in my daily relationship with God. It's a spiritual practice to express my own hopes and dreams, my own fears and sorrows—and those of others—in words of prayer. I'm simply a better man when I pray and when I write prayers. Writing prayers, poems, meditations and songs is my vehicle for expressing my mission of bringing holiness into the world through prayer.

I pray that you find meaning and comfort in these pages. I hope that my writing serves to draw individuals into a life of prayer. Perhaps some readers will even take up writing—essays, private letters to God, prayers or musings—as a spiritual practice. I also hope that this volume inspires you to pray in your own words. My wish is that you are inspired to pray in your own voice, from the depths of your own experiences, from the depths of your own heart.

———————

Prayer is an act of summoning light.
Blessing is an act of bending light.
Communion is the act of entering light.

Light is a universal metaphor for Divine energy, a symbol for holiness, truth, radiance, eminence, love. To pray is to summon Divine light into our lives. To bless is an attempt to summon that light and then to bend it toward holy purpose, including consolation, healing, joy and peace. Communion is the attempt to journey into the light of holiness, awe and wonder.

Think of this book as an invitation to prayer, an invitation to hope, an invitation to healing. Think of it as an invitation to bless yourself and others. Think of it as an invitation to take another step on the path toward entering the light of holiness, to redeem your moments of deepest sorrow, and to rejoice in your greatest moments of joy and love.

USING THESE PRAYERS

There are four classic voices of prayer: praise, petition, gratitude and forgiveness. These forms of prayer also have simpler, less theological names: "wow," "gimme," "thanks" and "oops." Many prayers, by their nature, include two or more of these voices. While all four categories are represented in this volume, the focus is on petition and gratitude.

Many of the structures of prayer used here will be very familiar to Jewish readers, such as personalizing prayers by adding an individual's name or adjusting a prayer to gender. Other aspects of these prayers may seem more foreign to Jews and more familiar to those of other faiths: in particular, customizing prayers with optional language. Jewish prayers tend to focus on a fixed liturgy for set times of prayer and specific blessings, called *brachot*, which are formulated blessings for specific instances, such as a blessing before a meal or a blessing to be said upon waking up. Even the prayer books used by the more liberal branches of Judaism contain fixed liturgies, albeit with optional alternative readings. Spontaneous personal prayer is not practiced in many Jewish prayer communities. Jewish prayer, however, remains deeply personal, with an emphasis on the internal attitude and approach during worship, known as *kavanah*.

The good news is that Judaism also has a long tradition of creating and using supplementary prayers of praise or petition, a tradition that has waxed and waned over the centuries. Saying a prayer with *kavanah*—with intention, understanding the words while being mindful of the prayer's inner meaning—is a central goal of all Jewish prayer. No matter the specific words, or whether the voice is "wow," "gimme," "thanks" or "oops," in prayer we're moving toward closeness to God.

PERSONALIZING THE PRAYERS

Many prayers in this volume are written to be personalized in a variety of ways, such as modifying the gender references, refining the emotional content via word choice and inserting names of individuals who are sick or in need of a blessing. The main symbols are brackets, slashes and blank lines. Here's a guide to the symbols that indicate choices for customizing the prayers.

Brackets [ ]: Brackets are found in these prayers for a variety of purposes, including: providing instructions for the person saying the prayer; identifying alternative paragraphs; providing optional language that reflects unique personal circumstances, such as specific words or phrases to include or omit; lists in which only one choice is needed; and lists in which some or all of the choices may be used, such as lists of emotions to refine feelings that are reflected in the prayer. The choices in these lists are separated by slashes.

Slashes /: Slashes typically denote: a gender choice, such as him/her; a choice to say the prayer in the first-person singular or the first-person plural, such as I/we; or a list of words for customizing the prayer, such as [brother/sister/friend] or [confusion/sorrow/anger/fear/doubt]. When two choices appear in a row, sets of brackets will follow each other—for example, [my/our] [son/daughter].

Blank lines _____: Blank lines are most commonly used to indicate the opportunity to insert an individual's name, typically in a healing prayer or a *Yizkor* prayer. A blank line can also indicate the opportunity to customize the prayer to an event. For example, "*Yizkor* for First Responders" can be customized to include the event in which the first responder died, such as [the 9/11 attacks on the United States, the Mount Carmel forest fire or other event]. In "*Yizkor* for a Soldier," there is the opportunity to name the war or conflict in which the soldier died. Occasionally, a blank line serves as an invitation for you to reflect on your own feelings and experiences as part of the prayer.

Hebrew words in the text of the prayers are in italics, except when that word has entered the English dictionary, such as Torah. A glossary of all Hebrew terms, whether or not they are in the English dictionary, appears at the end of this book.

INCLUDING AN INDIVIDUAL'S NAME IN A PRAYER

A common Jewish practice is to add an individual's name to prayers of healing and prayers of mourning, known as *Yizkor* prayers, and that custom has been added to a variety of the prayers in this volume. Adding an individual's name to a prayer can make it more personal and more meaningful. In Jewish prayer, an individual's Hebrew name takes on a very specific construct: the individual's first name followed by either "son of" or "daughter of" followed by one or both of the parents' first names. In this volume, the opportunity to include a person's name will be identified with a blank line followed by the instruction "[insert name]."

Healing prayers: In healing prayers, many Jews will use the first name of the individual who is sick and the mother's first name. Others use the individual's first name along with both the mother's and the father's names.

Yizkor **prayers:** Memorial prayers for specific individuals, known as *Yizkor* prayers, follow the same format, but either the father's first name—or both the father's and mother's first names—will be used. My personal practice, in all cases, is to use both the father's and the mother's first names. This is also a common egalitarian practice.

Unknown Hebrew name / other languages: If you don't know the individual's Hebrew name, or if the individual does not have one, add the person's name in your native tongue or the native tongue of the person you are remembering or for whom you are praying. Ideally, if you're praying for a Jew, find out his or her Hebrew name to use in the prayer. Don't be shy to ask the individual or a family member. Most people will be happy to know that you are saying a *bracha*—prayer, blessing—on their behalf. It may be that you don't know the individual's name, only the person's relationship to someone you know, such as a friend's grandmother. In such cases, identify the individual in a way that's most meaningful to you.

GOD'S NAME

Speaking and writing God's name carries weight, the weight of prayer, the weight of invoking holiness, the weight of summoning the Divine. It is not a casual business.

Jewish prayer addresses God in three ways: using God's personal, intimate names, such as *Adonai* and *Eloheinu*; with established titles for God used in *Tanach* (the Hebrew Bible), such as *Shomeir Yisrael* (Guardian of Israel) and *Tzur Yisrael* (Rock of Israel); and with more general descriptions of God, such as *tzuri v'go'ali* (my Rock and Redeemer). Prayers in this volume incorporate all three means of addressing God.

The Jewish names for God may be familiar to some readers. Perhaps they feel unfamiliar or uncomfortable to others. One goal of this book is to help people to pray authentically, from the heart. This is an invitation to those who are unfamiliar with the Jewish names for God to try using them, perhaps to refresh your relationship with the Creator. It's also an invitation for you to use names for God that are most comfortable for you when you are in private prayer. Use the name that most connects you to God in prayer.

Jews maintain a strong reverence for the names of God. In prayer, we use *"Adonai"* as the pronunciation of the tetragrammaton, the four-letter name of God, identified in the English alphabet as YHVH, since the actual pronunciation has been lost. *"Adonai"* literally means "the Lord." Over the centuries, this substitute pronunciation has taken on the weight of awe and reverence. This reverence is reflected in the written and spoken uses of God's name.

The Hebrew in this volume follows a common practice of substituting abbreviations and alternate spellings for names of God. *Adonai* is shown as the single Hebrew letter *hey* with an apostrophe: 'ה. *Eloheinu*, "our God," is slightly misspelled—as אלוקינו—substituting the ה with a ק. So is *Yah*, "God"—as קה—substituting the י with a ק. Along with reflecting reverence, these changes avoid an issue with Jewish law. Books that employ the full spelling of God's name in Hebrew cannot be casually treated or discarded. In adopting this practice, this volume is not considered sacred for Jewish purposes of use or disposal of holy books.

Among some Jews, this custom has drifted into English, with the practice of replacing the *o* in God with a dash, as follows: G-d. This is my practice when I write and when I post prayers on my website. I've seen other variations of this idea, with some people using "G!d" or "Gd." I do this as a personal reminder not to be casual in the use of God's name. For readability of this volume, however, I have opted to use the standard spelling.

CHATIMOT

Jewish prayers have a unique structure for ending a *bracha*, called a *chatima*. The word *chatima* literally means "seal." In classic Jewish prayer, the *chatima* begins "*Baruch atah Adonai . . .*" ("Blessed are You, *Adonai . . .*"). Roughly one-third of the prayers found in this volume end with a *chatima*. I've taken some of the *chatimot* from classic Jewish prayer. For example, several healing prayers end with a line from the morning service: "Blessed are You, *Adonai* our God, Ruler of the universe, who gives strength to the weary." I've written *chatimot* in English for many of the prayers in this book, working with translators to develop Hebrew.

Each of the *Yizkor* prayers presented here ends with the line: "May his/her soul be bound up in the bond of life, a living blessing in our midst." This is the translation of the Hebrew ending for the *Yizkor* prayers found in the *High Holiday Prayer Book* (Prayer Book Press of Media Judaica, 1978).

SUGGESTIONS FOR CLERGY

These prayers are written to be used in our daily lives. In addition, there are many potential uses for these prayers. Here's a list of suggestions for clergy to engage with these prayers:

- Use an individual prayer as a congregational handout during worship
- Provide copies of this book to congregants as part of counseling sessions
- Provide copies of individual prayers to congregants as part of counseling sessions
- Provide copies of this book as gifts at life-cycle events, such as births, *b'nei mitzvot*, weddings and other important family moments
- Provide copies of this book when visiting hospital, hospice, elder care, rehab or other settings
- Suggest that a congregant use one of these prayers as a reading at life-cycle events such as baby namings, circumcisions, *b'nei mitzvot*, weddings or funerals
- Use one of these prayers to open or close a sermon or a class, using the text to reinforce the message
- Use a prayer as the basis of a sermon or class, using the text as the basis of the talk or class in adult education, collegiate gatherings, day schools or Sunday school events
- Provide copies of individual prayers when visiting hospital, hospice, elder care, rehab or other settings
- Reprint an individual prayer in a congregational bulletin
- Use individual prayers in interfaith events, national commemorations and community gatherings

Please see www.tobendlight.com for reprint and copyright instructions, or e-mail me at alden@tobendlight.com.

Many prayers in this book and on my website were written at the suggestion of clergy from a variety of settings and religious backgrounds. Synagogue- and church-based clergy—as well clergy serving in pastoral care and teaching roles in hospice care, elder care and educational organizations—have suggested topics. This is an invitation for you to send me your suggestions for prayers that need to be written. I would also be happy to hear your stories of using these prayers. Please use the same e-mail address for your suggestions and stories.

A LIFE OF MEANING

HOPES

Seeking God

God of my ancestors,
God of generations,
God beyond my understanding:
Who are You?
What are You?
Where are You?
Why do I struggle to reach You
When my quiet heart already knows You?
My calm thoughts
And open arms
Already know You.
My joy and pain,
Grief and love
Already know You.

Adonai my God,
Open me up to You
In celebration and surrender.
Reunite me with what I already know:
Your holiness and Your love.
Let Your word flow through me,
So that I see and hear,
Taste, touch and smell,
The beauty and blessings around me.
Then, God of old,
I will remember to seek You always,
To praise You throughout the days,
And to honor You across the years.

Blessed are You,
Hidden in plain sight,
Present in simple moments,
Present for eternity.

בָּרוּךְ אַתָּה,
כָּמוּס בִּמְצִיאוּת גְּלוּיָה,
נוֹכֵחַ בִּרְגָעִים פְּשׁוּטִים,
נוֹכֵחַ לְנֶצַח נְצָחִים.

Baruch atah,
kamus bimtzi'ut g'luyah,
nochei'ach birga'im p'shutim,
nochei'ach l'netzach n'tzachim.

For Service

God of our fathers,
Abraham, Isaac and Jacob,
God of our mothers,
Sarah, Rebekah, Leah and Rachel,
Open my heart to serve others
With joy and thanksgiving.
Remove ego, judgment and self-will,
So that I am present with kindness and understanding.
Make me a tool of Your hand,
An echo of Your voice,
And a shining lamp of Your love.
Grant me the wisdom to offer myself willingly, without fear.
Fill me with compassion and grace,
Vitality and endurance,
So that my service becomes a blessing
In heaven and on earth.

Blessed are You, God of old,	בָּרוּךְ אַתָּה, אֱלֹקֵי כָּל הַזְּמַנִּים,
You set Your people	מוֹלִיךְ עַמְּךָ בְּדֶרֶךְ נֶאֱצֶלֶת,
on a noble path,	לְתַקֵּן עוֹלָם בְּאַהֲבָה.
To serve with love.	

Baruch atah, Elohei kol haz'manim,
molich am'cha b'derech ne'etzelet,
l'takein olam b'ahavah.

For Devotion

ה' שְׂפָתַי תִּפְתָּח, וּפִי יַגִּיד תְּהִלָּתֶךָ.

Adonai s'fatai tiftach, u'fi yagid t'hilatecha.

O Lord, open You my lips;
and my mouth shall declare Your praise.

—Psalms 51:17

God, open my lips, so that my mouth may declare Your
praise.
Open my mouth, so that my heart may sing Your glory.
Open my heart, so that my eyes may see Your wisdom.
Open my eyes, so that my soul feels Your presence.
Open my soul, so that my hands do Your mitzvot.
Open my hands, so that my works glorify Your Torah.
Open my works, so that my deeds bear witness to Your
truth.
Open my deeds, so that my life bears witness to Your justice.
Open my life, so that my spirit bears witness to Your mercy.
Open my spirit, so that my days declare Your Holy Name.

To Hear Your Voice

Divine voice of reason and love,
Of compassion and understanding:
    Speak gently and clearly, so that I may know Your will.
    Give me the patience to listen and the desire to seek
    Your counsel and instruction.
    Grant me the understanding to hear Your teachings in
        every voice,
    From all people,
    In every moment of need.
Open my heart to others,
To their suffering,
To their call for help.
Open my heart to love and laughter,
Song and dance,
Beauty and grace,
So that I remember to celebrate Your gifts day by day.

    Divine Creator of spirit and light,
    Teach me to hold my joys and sorrows gently in my
        hands
    And to honor them both.
    Teach me to be present to all that I see and all that I feel,
    In truth, without fear.
    Teach me to be present for others,
    In humble service.

Blessed are You,
Teacher and Guide,
You make Your wisdom known to those who ask
And those who listen, willingly and patiently,
To the voices of Your creation.

Blessed are You,   בָּרוּךְ אַתָּה, קוֹלְךָ מְהַדְהֵד בְּכָל הַבְּרִיאָה.
    Your voice resounds
    throughout creation.

Baruch atah, kol'cha m'hadheid b'chol hab'ri'ah.

To Seek Your Love

Divine Creator of beauty and light,
In wisdom You wait,
In love You hope,
In service You pray,
You pray for us to seek the radiance and splendor
Of the seen and unseen glories hidden in Your creation.
You pray for us to yearn for You,
As You yearn for us.

Holy One,
Ancient One,
Rock of life,
Let my thirst for You lead me on a righteous path,
On a path of joy and surrender,
A path of generous love.
Make me a witness to the constant flow of Divine gifts,
So that I remember to seek You in joy.

Blessed are You *Adonai*, בָּרוּךְ אַתָּה ה', הַשָּׂמֵחַ בְּאַהֲבַת עַמֶּךָ.
   delighting in Your
   people's love.

Baruch atah Adonai, hasamei'ach b'ahavat am'cha.

For Grace

All I am,
All I have,
All I'll become
Are present in this moment:
Warmth and breath,
Love and compassion,
Silence and celebration.
Everything, here.
All gifts, present.

What then, God of All Being,
What then of my choices?
What will I make of the space
Between this breath and the next?
Will I bring laughter and light,
Hope and faith,
Wonder and strength?
Will I stand in humble service
For all of my brothers and sisters?

Maker of heaven and earth,
Grant us the wisdom to choose lives of grace,
Lives of vision and understanding,
Seeing each moment as a choice
To bless our companions
With strength and wisdom,
With honor and respect.

Blessed are the gentle   מְבֹרָכִים רִגְעֵי הַחֶסֶד הָרַכִּים.
  moments of grace.

M'vorachim rig'ei hachesed harakim.

Prayers of My Heart

God of millennia,
God of generations
And the great expanse,
I have but a moment,
A flicker of time to
Bless and be blessed.

These are the prayers of my heart:
Tenderness and Shabbat.
The spiritual practice of love.
To know and not to know.
To be strong in faith and open to adventure.
To laugh in the wind.
To smile in the sunshine.
To play in the rain.
To live in dignity.
To consecrate the hours.
To sanctify my days.
To live Your Torah.
To praise Your name.
Shabbat and tenderness.
The spiritual practice of love.

The Path of Righteousness

God of what was and what will be,
    Of what might have been and might still be.
God of past and future,
    Of memories and beginnings.
God of the finite and the infinite,
    Of moments and possibilities.
What is my life?
    And what of my death?
What of my choices?
    And what of my future?
What of this distance?
    And what of the endless sky?
What of the darkness?
    And what of the light?

God of the seen and unseen,
    Of the known and unknowable.
Teach me patience and understanding
    As the mysteries of my life unfold.
Teach me to live gently, love generously,
    And to walk with strength and confidence.
Teach me to give and to receive,
    Sharing Your blessings in joy and sorrow.
Teach me to see others through Your eyes,
    As children of God.
And teach me to see myself and my life as You do,
    With love.

<table>
<tr><td>Blessed are You, Adonai,</td><td dir="rtl">בָּרוּךְ אַתָּה ה',</td></tr>
<tr><td>Source of life,</td><td dir="rtl">מְקוֹר חַיִּים,</td></tr>
<tr><td>Guardian and Shelter,</td><td dir="rtl">שׁוֹמֵר וּמָגֵן,</td></tr>
<tr><td>You set Your people on the</td><td dir="rtl">מוֹלִיךְ עַמְּךָ בְּדֶרֶךְ צֶדֶק,</td></tr>
<tr><td>path of righteousness,</td><td dir="rtl">קְדֻשָּׁה וּצְדָקָה,</td></tr>
<tr><td>Holiness and charity,</td><td dir="rtl">חֵן וָחֶסֶד,</td></tr>
<tr><td>Kindness and grace,</td><td dir="rtl">לָשׁוּב אֵלֶיךָ לְתַקֵּן עוֹלָם בְּמַלְכוּת שַׁקַּי.</td></tr>
<tr><td>To return to You in service.</td><td dir="rtl">בָּרוּךְ שִׁמְךָ הַקָּדוֹשׁ.</td></tr>
<tr><td>Blessed is Your Holy Name.</td><td></td></tr>
</table>

Baruch atah Adonai,
m'kor chayim,
shomeir u'magein,
molich am'cha b'derech tzedek,
k'dushah u'tz'dakah,
chein vachesed,
lashuv eilecha l'takein olam b'malchut Shadai.
Baruch shimcha hakadosh.

Offerings

When God offers love, I offer my heart.
When God offers wisdom, I offer my mind.
When God offers beauty, I offer my senses.
When God offers silence, I offer my patience.
When God offers challenge, I offer my strength.
When God offers trial, I offer my faith.
When God offers pain, I offer my dignity.
When God offers fear, I offer my courage.
When God offers grief, I offer my endurance.
When God offers shame, I offer my amends.
When God offers death, I offer my mourning.
When God offers life, I offer my rejoicing.
When God offers joy, I offer my thanksgiving.
When God offers awe, I offer my wonder.
When God offers righteousness, I offer my blessings.
When God offers holiness, I offer my praise.

For Humility

God, give me a quiet heart,
A peaceful heart,
A humble heart.

Teach me to be gentle with myself,
So that I may be gentle with others.
Teach me to be patient with myself,
So that I may be patient with others.
Teach me kindness and gratitude,
Joy and humor,
Strength and forgiveness,
Trust and faith,
Openness, willingness and surrender.

To praise, not to be praised.
To bless, not to be blessed.
To glorify, not to be glorified.
To extol, not to be extolled.
To sanctify, not to be sanctified.

So that all will go well with Your people Israel.

For Compassion

The man in the gutter,
The woman on the street,
They are my sister and my brother.

The frail and the meek,
The lonely and the lost,
They are my father and my mother.

The soldier under fire,
The girl in a wheelchair,
They are my son and my daughter.

The widow and the orphan,
The confused and the lost,
They are my cousins and my friends.

God of justice,
Only You know why one man is born for silk
And another man is born for sand.
Only You know why one woman is born for castles
And another is born for cardboard.

God of mercy,
Grant me the wisdom and compassion
To see all men and women
As my family and kin.
Help me to use the gifts of my life
As blessings to share.
Grant me compassion for those in need:
The suffering, the hungry,
Those in pain,
Those in fear.
Lead me to a path
Of love and healing
In service to Your Holy Name.

For Joy

Listen with your eyes
And hear with your heart:
In every grief, there is blessing . . .
    In every joy, there is hope . . .
In every love, thanksgiving . . .
    In every thought, wisdom . . .
In every breath, renewal . . .
    In every moment, a choice,
    To stay bent in sorrow,
    Or to lift ourselves in songs of praise
To God Most High.
    To dance with Miriam.
To dream with Jacob.
    To laugh with Sarah.
To greet angels with Abraham.
    To argue with heaven on behalf of earth.

God of the seen and unseen,
Creator of light and darkness,
Author of justice and mercy,
Give us the courage and strength to choose a life of service,
Guided by Your loving hand,
A life of song and dance,
Gentleness and peace,
Honor and grace,
Kindness and understanding.

Blessed are You, *Adonai*   בָּרוּךְ אַתָּה ה' אֱלֹקֵינוּ, אוֹהֵב
    our God, You love   שִׂמְחָה וְשָׂמֵחַ בְּתִקּוּן הָעוֹלָם.
    joy and service.

Baruch atah Adonai Eloheinu, oheiv
simchah v'samei'ach b'tikun ha'olam.

For a New Vision

With new vision
We see the abundance of Your world,
Blessings of heaven and earth.

God, help us to see the world through Your eyes,
And one another,
And ourselves.
For joy and peace,
For love and light,
That we may bring holiness into Your world.

Blessed are You, *Adonai*,　　　　　בָּרוּךְ אַתָּה ה',
God of all worlds,　　　　　　　רִבּוֹן כָּל הָעוֹלָמִים,
Who creates moments when　בּוֹרֵא רְגָעִים בָּהֶם שָׁמַיִם נוֹשְׁקִים לָאָרֶץ,
　　heaven touches earth,　　מַתִּיר לָנוּ לִשְׁמֹעַ דְּבָרְךָ,
Allowing us to hear　　　　　　לָחוּשׁ אֶת אוֹרְךָ
　　Your word,　　　　　　וְלַחֲזוֹת בַּזִּיו הָאֱלֹקִי.
To feel Your radiance
And to see Your Divine light.

Baruch atah Adonai,
Ribon kol ha'olamim,
borei r'ga'im bahem shamayim nosh'kim la'aretz,
matir lanu lishmo'a d'var'cha,
lachush et or'cha
v'lachazot baziv ha'Elohi.

Each Day

To start this day with joy.
To end this day with peace.
To start this day with longing.
To end this day released.

Live each day with valor,
With trust, with hope, with faith.
Live each day with wonder,
With kindness, awe and grace.

Hold fast to sacred moments.
Hold fast to precious love.
Hold fast to one another.
Hold fast to God above.

Hold courage through the hours,
And humor through the tears.
Hold God above your sorrows.
Hold God above your fears.

To You I must surrender,
Oh God of hidden spheres.
You are Source and Shelter.
To You I pledge my years.

PRAISES

For Creation

Author of life,
Architect of creation,
Artist of earth,
Your works declare Your Holy Name.

Mighty rivers,
Turbulent seas,
Towering mountains,
Rolling hills,
Vast spaces of brilliance and grandeur.

You created palette and paint,
Color and hue,
Shape and form,
Abundant and beautiful,
Glorious and majestic,
Full of mystery and wonder.

Blessed are You,
With Divine love You
   created a world
   of splendor.

בָּרוּךְ אַתָּה,
בְּאַהֲבָה שְׁמֵימִית בָּרֵאתָ
עוֹלָם שֶׁל הוֹד וְהָדָר.

Baruch atah,
b'ahavah sh'meimit barata olam shel hod v'hadar.

18

In Praise

Hallelujah at sunset.
Hallelujah at daybreak.
Hallelujah at dusk.
Hallelujah at dawn.
Hallelujah with pauper and prince,
With beggar and king.
Hallelujah with all God's works.

This is my prayer, God of Sarah,
To declare Your glory in all things.

Hallelujah in sunshine.
Hallelujah in shadow.
Hallelujah in calm.
Hallelujah in storm.
Hallelujah in peace.
Hallelujah at war.
Hallelujah in shelter.
Hallelujah when all comfort and protection
Appear lost.

This is our prayer, God of Abraham,
To praise You every moment.
To praise You,
To sing to You,
To dance for You,
To declare hallelujah with our lives.

Sing Hallelujah

Hallelujah
A hymn of glory,
A chant of praise,
A song of thanksgiving.
Voices raised, hearts to heaven.
Lungs full and strong,
A breath, a note, a lyric, a tune.
A call of love,
An echo of truth,
Resounding with joy and praise.

Let my hopes carry me toward wondrous deeds.
Let my heart lead me toward sacred wisdom.
Let my breath lead me toward majestic truth.
Let my words exalt Your Holy Name.

Hallelujah
A song of hope,
A harmony of justice,
A chorus of mercy.

God of Miriam,
Prophet who danced by the sea,
Teach me the song of life,
Of dedication and zeal,
Of wonder and glory.
Teach me to sing my hallelujah.
Teach me to live my hallelujah.
A song of righteousness,
A song of thanksgiving,
A song for the generations.

Dance Hallelujah

Hallelujah
A dance of wonder,
A dance of joy and thanksgiving.
Arms raised, hands to the sky,
Feet solid, connected to earth.
A step, a bend, a twirl, a leap.
A breath of light,
A stream of color,
Spinning toward radiance and splendor.

Let my feet lead me toward Your holy realm.
Let my legs carry me toward Your Divine word.
Let my arms lift praises toward Your marvelous works.
Let my body exclaim the power of Your awesome ways.

Hallelujah
A dance of light and love,
A dance of energy and endurance,
A dance of humility and grace.

God of Miriam,
Prophet who danced by the sea,
Teach me the dance of awe and mystery,
Of devotion and ecstasy,
Of passion and praise.
Teach me to dance my hallelujah.
Teach me to live my hallelujah.
A dance of radiance,
A dance of splendor,
A dance of peace.

Praise the New Day

Praise the new day,
A gift of the Source of All Being,
The breath of life,
The soul of the universe.
Cherish the moments
And sanctify the hours.
Bless the joys
And honor the tears.
Lift your heart in song.
Raise your voice in thanksgiving.
Magnify your faith.
Practice acceptance.
Offer consolation.
Seek wisdom.
Become a well of healing,
A beacon of kindness,
A source of forgiveness,
A light of wonder and wisdom.

Soul of the universe,
Breath of life,
Source of All Being,
We praise the new day.
A gift of holiness and love.

Sing Out

When you feel the light of holiness,
The radiance of love,
The shimmering of glory,
The luminous glow of spirit . . .

When you inhale wonder
And exhale awe . . .

When mystery and majesty flow
Through your pulsing veins . . .

When God's whisper becomes a thundering
Blast of the shofar . . .

When your soul remembers its
Place in the heavens . . .

Sing out!
Sing out your joy.
Sing out your praise.

When you feel the light of Torah,
The radiance of mitzvot,
The shimmering of prayer,
The luminous glow of loving-kindness . . .

Sing out!
Sing out to God.
Your voice will join the chorus of angels,
And your heart will know
The secret of eternity.

Every Heart

Let us exalt
Your Holy Name,
Proclaiming Your majesty,
Proclaiming Your sovereignty,
Proclaiming Your splendor.
Let our limbs announce Your radiance,
And our voices declare Your glory.
Let us sing and shout,
So that the hills echo with praise,
And the streets pulse with prayer,
So that the seas swell with rejoicing,
And the cities vibrate with thanksgiving.
Then the universe will expand with wonder,
And the heavenly host will join in the song.
The gates of righteousness will burst open.
The path to mystery will shine.
The way to holiness will sparkle.
The route to beauty will gleam.
Every heart will turn to You,
Adonai our God,
In joyous surrender.
Every heart will know gratitude and love,
Happiness and consolation.
Justice and mercy will reign,
And peace will hallow the earth.

Your Name

God of old,
Your name is Peace.
Your name is Justice.
Your name is Mercy.

God of life,
Your name is Compassion.
Your name is Love.
Your name is Hope.

God of blessing,
Your name is Truth.
Your name is Wisdom.
Your name is Righteousness.

God of our fathers,
God of our mothers,
Your name is in my heart
And before my eyes.

Blessed are You, *Adonai*,　　　בָּרוּךְ אַתָּה ה', שִׁמְךָ זוֹרֵחַ בְּכָל הַבְּרִיאָה.
Your name shines
　　throughout creation.

Baruch atah Adonai, shimcha zorei'ach b'chol hab'ri'ah.

FAMILY

Father's Meditation

Gracious and Compassionate One,
Mother of the Universe,
Father of Life,
Source and Shelter,
Hear this prayer:

My children are Yours,
To guide and protect with Your strong hand,
To care for and nurture with Your outstretched arm,
To hold and heal with Your righteous ways.
Grant them vitality and fortitude
As they build lives of their own.
Fill their days with meaning and purpose,
Joy and adventure,
Thanksgiving and peace.
Ease their burdens and relieve their struggles.
Grant them years of prosperity and serenity,
Wisdom and courage,
Gratitude and wonder.
May they enjoy the fruits of Your creation
In service to Torah and our people Israel.

Blessed are You, *Adonai* our God,   בָּרוּךְ אַתָּה ה' אֱלֹקֵינוּ,
God of our ancestors,   אֱלֹקֵי אֲבוֹתֵינוּ וְאִמּוֹתֵינוּ,
God of generations.   אֱלֹקֵי הַדּוֹרֹת.

Baruch atah Adonai Eloheinu,
Elohei avoteinu v'imoteinu,
Elohei hadorot.

Mother's Meditation

Gracious and Compassionate One,
Father of the Universe,
Mother of Life,
Fountain and Well,
Hear this prayer:

My children are Yours,
To guide and protect with Your open hand,
To care for and nurture with Your wisdom,
To hold and heal with Your loving ways.
Grant them vitality and fortitude
As they build lives of their own.
Fill their days with friendship and hope,
Joy and kindness,
Thanksgiving and peace.
Shield them from pain and strife.
Grant them years of prosperity and serenity,
Gratitude and faith,
Awe and wonder.
May they enjoy the fruits of Your creation
In service to Torah and our people Israel.

Blessed are You, *Adonai* our God,	בָּרוּךְ אַתָּה ה' אֱלֹקֵינוּ,
God of our ancestors,	אֱלֹקֵי אֲבוֹתֵינוּ וְאִמּוֹתֵינוּ,
God of generations.	אֱלֹקֵי הַדּוֹרוֹת.

Baruch atah Adonai Eloheinu,
Elohei avoteinu v'imoteinu,
Elohei hadorot.

For Family

God of generations,
Source of hope,
Flame of forgiveness,
Bless our family with kindness and respect,
Compassion and grace,
And the wisdom to heal the wounds of time.

Make me a brother/sister to my [brother(s) and sister(s)]
    [siblings],
A son/daughter to my [father/mother/parents/stepmother/
    stepfather],
A father/mother to my [son(s)/daughter(s)] and
A friend to my friends.
Give me the understanding and willingness
To be present in their moments of joy and grief,
Just as I pray that they will be present for mine.
Help me to forgive their weaknesses,
Just as I pray that they will forgive mine.
[For those who have harmed me, let me hold no anger or
    malice.]
May our bond [remain/become] powerful and sustaining
And our kinship a rock of support and strength.
Let love echo through my words
And dedication shine through my deeds.
Let my life become a testimony to the longings and
    aspirations
Of our ancestors.

Blessed are You, *Adonai* our God,	בָּרוּךְ אַתָּה ה' אֱלֹקֵינוּ,
With love You gave us the	נָתַתָּ לָנוּ בְּמַתָּנָה אֶת
gift of each other.	זוּלָתֵנוּ בְּאַהֲבָה.

Baruch atah Adonai Eloheinu,
natata lanu b'matanah et zulateinu b'ahavah.

On the Birth of a Child

Precious child,
Wonder of creation,
You are proof of Divine love,
Witness to our Maker's glory,
Witness to the blessed partnership
Between woman, man and God.
What makes me worthy of you?
What makes me able to gently guide you on your sacred
    path,
Your own journey to wisdom, charity, righteousness and
    Torah?

Father of the universe,
Mother of creation,
Be my guide and teacher,
As I father/mother/parent this new life,
This precious gift.
Give me humility, compassion and wisdom
To teach her/him Torah and mitzvot
Through my actions and my life,
So that we become each other's blessings.

Gracious God, be my partner in raising this child,
For this gift is not mine.
It is ours to nurture, to grow,
And to give back to the world for *tikun olam*.

On the Birth of Grandchildren

In gratitude and thanksgiving,
Humbly and on bended knee,
We offer praise to You,
God Most High,
For the gift of grandchildren.
Bless them with prosperity and health,
Wisdom and strength,
Grace and happiness.
Bless them with well-being
And a sense of well-being.
May they thirst for Torah and mitzvot,
And do honor to Your Holy Name.

Bless their parents with patience and understanding.
Bless their grandparents with joy and devotion.
Bless them at home,
Bless them on their way.
Bless them in study,
Bless them at play.
Bless them in love,
Bless them in heartache.
Shelter them,
Guide them,
Protect them,
Heal them in their time of need.
God of our ancestors,
Source and comfort,
Love them as You love Your people Israel.

Blessed are You,	בָּרוּךְ אַתָּה,
Creator of All,	יוֹצֵר הַכּל,
Father of Kindness,	אַב הַחֶסֶד,
Mother of Wisdom,	אֵם הַחָכְמָה,
Gentle Teacher,	מוֹרֶה עָדִין,
You renew Your people	הַמְחַדֵּשׁ עַמְּךָ בְּחַיִּים חֲדָשִׁים,
with new life, new	בְּאַהֲבָה חֲדָשָׁה,
love, new birth,	בְּלֵדָה חֲדָשָׁה,
Generation after generation,	מִדּוֹר לְדוֹר,
In love.	בְּאַהֲבָה.

Baruch atah,
yotzeir hakol,
av hachesed,
eim hachochmah,
moreh adin,
ham'chadeish am'cha b'chayim chadashim,
b'ahavah chadashah,
b'leidah chadashah,
midor l'dor,
b'ahavah.

For the Matriarch

For our matriarch,
  A song of strength and hope.

Guardian of generations,
Keeper of traditions,
Hand of guidance and love,
We are blessed by your wisdom and purpose,
Your work to bind us to our heritage,
Your dedication to peace in our homes
And joy in our lives.
You remind us to open our hearts to our brothers and sisters,
Fathers and mothers,
Daughters and sons.
You remind us to honor and cherish cousins of cousins of
  cousins,
And to live together, in harmony,
By God's holy word.

God of motherly wisdom and grace,
Bless our family with health
And our matriarch with vision, endurance and hope.
May her devotion inspire us to live by our highest ideals,
Guided by Torah.
Bless our lives with laughter
And our days with purpose,
So that we bring radiance and splendor to our family
And to the world.

Blessed are You, God   בָּרוּךְ אַתָּה,
  of our mothers,   קֵל אִמּוֹתֵינוּ,
Who provides just and   בּוֹרֵא נָשִׁים יְשָׁרוֹת וְצַדִּיקוֹת
  righteous women   בְּכָל דּוֹר וָדוֹר.
In every generation.

Baruch atah, El imoteinu,
borei nashim y'sharot v'tzadikot
b'chol dor vador.

For the Patriarch

For our patriarch,
    A song of dignity and honor.

Guardian of mitzvot,
Keeper of truths,
Hand of protection and peace,
We are blessed with your humor and compassion,
Your zest for life
And your zeal for family.
You remind us to open our lives to God's majesty and
    mystery,
God's justice and mercy.
You remind us to seek radiance and splendor,
Awe for creation and compassion for each other,
And choose joy over grief,
Laughter over tears.

God of fatherly patience and strength,
Bless our family with love
And our patriarch with vision, endurance and hope.
May his devotion inspire us to righteousness and charity,
Guided by Torah.
Bless our lives with abundance
And our days with vigor,
So that we bring majesty and mystery to our lives
And into the world.

Blessed are You, God   בָּרוּךְ אַתָּה,
    of our fathers,   אֵל אֲבוֹתֵינוּ,
Who provides just and   בּוֹרֵא גְּבָרִים יְשָׁרִים וְצַדִּיקִים
    righteous men   בְּכָל דּוֹר וָדוֹר.
In every generation.

Baruch atah, El avoteinu,
borei g'varim y'sharim v'tzadikim
b'chol dor vador.

For Our Sisters

For our sisters,
    A dance of joy.

Sister, to have you is a blessing,
A gift of grace and love.
Your dignity is my shield,
Your compassion, my cloak,
Your wisdom, my guide,
Your laughter, my hope.
Your triumphs witness your endurance,
Your purpose,
Your power.

You are my sister by birth,
My sister by choice,
My sister through heartache,
My sister through blessings.

God of sisterly devotion and warmth,
Bless our family with understanding
And our sisters with passion, prosperity and peace.
May their devotion inspire us to kindness and service.
Bless our days with moments together,
Celebrations of love and loss,
So that we may bring renewal and rejoicing into our lives
And into the world.

Blessed are You, God   בָּרוּךְ אַתָּה, קֵל הָאֲחָיוֹת,
    of sisters,   הַשָּׂמֵחַ בְּאַהֲבַת אֲחָיוֹת.
Who delights in sisterly love.

Baruch atah, El ha'achayot,
hasamei'ach b'ahavat achayot.

For Our Brothers

For our brothers,
   A chant of honor.

Brother, to have you is a blessing,
A gift of endurance and strength.
Your courage is my shield,
Your humor, my cloak,
Your humility, my guide,
Your vigor, my hope.
Your victories witness your confidence,
Your devotion,
Your zeal.

You are my brother by birth
My brother by choice,
My brother through pain,
My brother in thanksgiving.

God of brotherly dignity and grace,
Bless our family with gratitude
And our brothers with enthusiasm, vitality and wonder.
May their devotion inspire us to justice and mercy.
Bless our lives with energy and prosperity,
So that we become a source of healing in our lives
And in the world.

Blessed are You, God   בָּרוּךְ אַתָּה, קֵל הָאַחִים,
   of brothers,   הַשָּׂמֵחַ בְּאַהֲבַת אַחִים.
Who delights in
   brotherly love.

Baruch atah, El ha'achim,
hasamei'ach b'ahavat achim.

For the Family Historian

For the family historian,
    A song of thanksgiving.

Guardian of the family tree,
Keeper of our history,
We are blessed with your love and devotion,
Your tireless efforts to know our heritage,
Your work to keep us united,
Your joy in rediscovering brothers and sisters
Once separated, apart no more.
Your work reminds us to love and cherish the living,
To honor and praise the dead,
To embrace the lost,
To welcome one another home.

God of mystery and wonder,
Bless our family with strength and peace,
Wholeness and love,
Health and prosperity.
May sons and daughters find joy under the chuppah.
May our parents be given long lives and easy deaths.
Bless us with children, grandchildren and great-grandchildren,
So that the generations expand,
A wondrous celebration of Your gifts.

Blessed are You, God of our
    mothers and fathers,
Who delights in family
    wholeness and love.

בָּרוּךְ אַתָּה, קֵל אֲבוֹתֵינוּ וְאִמּוֹתֵינוּ,
הַמִּתְעַנֵּג עַל אַחְדוּת וְאַהֲבָה בַּמִּשְׁפָּחָה.

*Baruch atah, El avoteinu v'imoteinu,
hamit'aneig al achdut v'ahavah bamishpachah.*

Meditation for a Child's First Torah Reading

Holy One,
Ancient Source of wisdom and truth,
My daughter/son is about to enter
The sacred garden of Your law,
Chanting Torah on behalf of our people for the first time.
How splendid is this moment!
How amazing in beauty and hope!
May this be the beginning of a miraculous journey,
A sacred romance of head and heart
Between my daughter/son and the wisdom of the ages,
Between my child and Your holy word.
Grant me the ability to listen and to hear
As she/he gives voice to Your mysteries.
May this moment herald a life
Dedicated to unlocking the secrets
Hidden in our holy texts.
May I be privileged to hear her/him
Read Torah again and again,
Always remembering my joy in this moment,
My heart full of praises.

My Child Leaves Home

Holy One,
Heavenly Guide,
My daughter/son is leaving home
To begin the adventure of an independent life.
Bless her/his journey with joy and wonder.
Let opportunity open like a rose before her/his eyes.
Be her/his compass and her/his shield.
Lead her/him on a path of discovery
Guided by the love of Torah,
A commitment to mitzvot,
And dedication to the Jewish people.
Bless her/him with mentors and teachers,
Companions and friends,
Scholars and rabbis,
To support and guide her/him along the way.

In this marvel,
In this glorious moment of growth fulfilled,
My heart struggles with contradictions:
Pride and fear,
Joy and grief,
Love and loss.
The landscape of my life is shifting,
Offering new challenges and new choices
In the very moment my child departs.
Give me the wisdom and strength to honor my own life
With gentleness and courage,
And to embrace the beauty and promise of the time to come.

God of our fathers and mothers,
God of sacred transitions,
Bless my daughter/son
_____ [insert child's name]
As she/he sets out on this new life.
Keep her/him safe under a canopy of peace.
May she/he be a blessing to her/his [new] community.
Lead us back to each other often,
With stories of marvelous moments and amazing discovery.

Blessed are You, *Adonai*   בָּרוּךְ אַתָּה ה' אֱלֹקֵינוּ,
    our God,   הַמָּגֵן עַל חַיֵּי יְלָדֵינוּ.
Who watches over the
    lives of our children.

Baruch atah Adonai Eloheinu,
hamagein al chayei y'ladeinu.

Family Healing

God of old,
Our family has been fractured,
Torn apart by _____ [anger/violence/death/
    alcoholism/suicide/disease/fear/confusion/mental illness/
    rape/incest/neglect/abandonment],
Old wounds that have seeped into our bones and our blood,
Our thoughts and our words.
Release me from my anger and my guilt,
So I may see my kin with new eyes—
Their losses and fears,
Their pain and shame—
And therefore find a source of
Forgiveness and renewed love.

Well of blessings,
Lead us to new vision and new wisdom,
The place where love rests safely in our hearts
And peace waits quietly in our hands.

God of generations,
Grant healing to my family, speedily,
So that we may rejoice together in Your gifts,
With joy and thanksgiving.

Dear Brother, Dear Sister

How long,
Dear brother,
How long has it been
Since we saw each other?
Stood together?
Wept upon each other's necks?

How long,
Dear sister,
How long has it been
Since we embraced?
Shared stories?
Shed tears of joy and affection?

Come, let me hold you.
Come, let me hear you.
Come, let me see you.

And this moment will be for gladness.
This moment will be for blessing.
This moment will be for service.
And this moment will be for love.

Blessed are You,　　　　　בָּרוּךְ אַתָּה,
God of our fathers　　　אֱלֹקֵי אֲבוֹתֵינוּ וְאִמּוֹתֵינוּ,
　　and mothers,　　הַשָּׂמֵחַ בְּאִחוּד מִשְׁפָּחוֹת.
You rejoice when
　　families unite.

Baruch atah,
Elohei avoteinu v'imoteinu,
hasamei'ach b'ichud mishpachot.

LOVE AND FRIENDSHIP

For New Love

God of mystery and majesty,
Creator of redemption and hope,
I give thanks for the gift of new love.
Grant me the gentleness and courage,
The bravery and patience,
To let this love unfold like a flower,
A source of wonder and beauty
To be nurtured, blessed, praised and cherished
For what it is in this moment:
A seed with tiny imperceptible roots
And the beginning of a fragile stem hidden within.
It may take hold—and this would be beautiful—
Or it may wash away, which is the nature of some things.
This seed has so much energy,
So much God-given yearning for life,
Yearning to hold fast in the cradle of earth,
Yearning to reach for warmth and light,
That it may yield a meadow,
A sea of wildflowers,
Perhaps fragile,
Perhaps sturdy,
Always seeking light and air and earth.
Or it may disappear in the wind.

Heavenly source of radiance and splendor,
Let this new love be a blessing.
Give it strong roots to stay planted firmly against the
    elements
And a hearty stalk to bend gracefully with the seasons.

You who know the deepest mysteries of the heart,
May our moments together yield blessings for us
And for everyone we meet.

Blessed are You, Source
    of blessing and love.

בָּרוּךְ אַתָּה, מְקוֹר הַבְּרָכָה וְהָאַהֲבָה.

Baruch atah, m'kor hab'rachah v'ha'ahavah.

For an Open Heart

God, give me an open heart,
A generous heart,
A humble heart.
Give me a heart so free,
So fearless,
That I offer love without requirement,
To love as You love,
Holding my beloved precious,
Loving her/him in this moment exactly as she/he is,
Praying that she/he follows her/his true path
Regardless of where it takes her/him.

Give me a heart gentle and willing to love her/him
As she/he would be loved, with honor and respect,
Kindness and humor,
Joy and friendship.
Give me a love so pure and vast,
So simple and strong,
That it cherishes the love and the loving,
Asking nothing in return.

In This Turning: A New Year's Day Meditation

Darkness and grace
Mourning and thunder
Light and rejoicing
Daybreak and open sky

Here I surrender
To the chance for love
Your warm breath
Your loving hands
The fire in your eyes
The hope in your heart

What gifts wait in this turning
To you
To myself
This joy
This adventure

What gifts wait in this turning
And this yearning
This new year
This new wonder

Let blessings rain down
Upon me/us from heaven
And let hope settle softly
Upon this open heart

Let this be the time to sing
To dance
To play
And to delight in another
Glorious
Day

Quick Blessing for a Past Love

Light from my past,
You were once the joy of my present
And the hope of our future.
I remember you with affection
And pray that you have found
Joy and contentment
Prosperity and peace.
Your heart and your gentle hand
Remain a source of gentle warmth
Even as the rhythm of our lives
Moves in separate directions.
May you dwell in the tent of health and happiness
Secure in a life of friendship and love
Rejoicing in a life of awe and wonder.

This Ring: An Ending

When I put your ring on my finger
I wrapped it around my heart.

In removing this ring from my finger
I release my heart
With grief and joy,
Uncertainty and faith,
In unequal measures.

Ancient One,
God of compassion and grace,
Let this moment be a blessing,
So that healing continues
To flow into my hours and days.
Grant me the strength and insight
To honor the past and embrace the future
With dignity and passion,
Wisdom and thanksgiving,
Kindness and charity.
Then, God of wholeness and healing,
I will return to song and dance,
Laughter and praise,
As a beacon of Your light,
A source of joy, hope and love.

This Ring: An Ending (long version)

When I put your ring on my finger
I wrapped it around my heart.
A dream fulfilled.
A moment ripe with potential.

In removing this ring from my finger
I release my heart
With grief and joy,
Uncertainty and faith,
In unequal measures.

[Remove ring; set it aside or hand it to someone, the reverse
   of the wedding process.]

Ancient One,
God of compassion and grace,
Let this moment be a blessing,
So that healing continues
To flow into my hours and days.

[Grant my children
Comfort and relief,
Solace and understanding,
In the days and weeks ahead.
Let me be a source of strength and consolation for them,
An unbroken source of love.]

Grant me the insight
To honor the past and embrace the future
With dignity and passion,
Wisdom and thanksgiving,
Kindness and charity.
Then, God of life,
I will return in wholeness
To a life of joy,
To song and dance,
Laughter and praise,
As a beacon of Your light,
A source of hope and peace.

On Connecting with Old Friends

Fantastic. Amazing. Wonderful.
Frightening. Adventurous. Astounding.
My dear friend _____ [insert name]
Has returned to my life after [years/decades/an eternity]
Of time and distance.
Help me to see the gifts we bring to each other—
The stories, the history, the moments of joy and
     companionship,
The challenges, the losses, the moments of pain and
     sorrow—
As a source of Your Divine wisdom and love.

Why now?
What lessons are here for me?
What memories will come galloping back into my heart?

God of mystery and wonder,
Grant me the wisdom to listen to this messenger of
     friendship and love.
Make this a moment of gentleness and understanding,
A moment of grace and forgiveness,
So that our lives are renewed to each other
In joy and thanksgiving.
May this reunion be a blessing to us both.

Quick Blessing for a Friend's Departure

Heart of my heart,
Dear brother/sister/friend,
Bless you on your journey.
May you find what you seek
And what you need,
What seeks you
And what calls you home.
May the light of health and hope
Carry you toward beauty and wonder.
May the light of holiness
Carry you toward strength and service.
Let peace and joy surround your days.
And let awe and thanksgiving
Lead you on a path of virtue.

MEDITATIONS NEAR THE END OF LIFE

Near the End: A Meditation

When my days fade,
When my eyes dim,
When darkness settles,
And the veil is lifted,
Remove my fear,
My doubt,
My shame.
Remove my hesitation and longings,
So I may go gracefully into
The unknown,
The unknowable,
The secret tomorrow of my soul.

Ancient One,
Foundation and Shelter,
Companion and Guide,
Cradle of life,
Guardian of spirit,
I confess my weaknesses and mistakes,
My errors of judgment and
My lapses of conscience,
So that I may return to You in joyous surrender.

Source of my life,
Holy and exalted,
You have called me to service on this earth.
You will call me back to You
As You call all Your children
To return from this life,
This journey,
This place of sea and sky,
Of happiness and heartbreak.
Let me go in peace.
Let me go in peace.

Things Break

Things break. Things die.
People break. People die.
The end approaches
Sometimes swiftly,
Sometimes slowly,
Sometimes secretly,
Sometimes in plain sight.

Things thrive. Things live.
People thrive. People live.
Vitality flows from the heavens.
Energy reaches up from the core of the earth.
Love shines from the center of my heart.

God of time and space,
All beginnings lead to endings.
All endings are beginnings.
Grant me the wisdom to see life as a sea
Of losses and gains,
A tide of joy and heartache,
Birth and death,
Illness and recovery,
The sacred and the profane.

God of All,
Glorious and holy,
Things thrive, things break.
People live, people die.
Your love is eternal.

God of All, Your love
   is eternal.

קֵל הַכּל, אַהֲבַתְךָ נִצְחִית.

El hakol, ahavat'cha nitzchit.

Every Beginning

Every beginning brings an ending.
Every ending brings a beginning.

Ancient One,
This is the joy and the grief,
The plenty and the famine,
The dance and the dirge
Of life
Alive and awake
In Your world.

How wonderful is this living?
How glorious the light from heaven?
How stunning the radiance that surrounds You
My beloved,
Holy and new, luminous with wonder?
How marvelous this place where earth and sky touch?

How strange is this dying?
How melancholy that one day we will
No longer hear sweet voices,
See sweet faces,
Share whispers and secrets,
Laughter and heartbreak?
How much more, my darlings,
Should we love today?
How much more, my children,
Should we savor and rejoice?

Every beginning brings an ending.
Every ending brings a beginning.

Blessed is God's Holy Name.

Dwelling Place

This is my dwelling place.
The place of my bounty and sustenance,
Study and reflection.

This is my living place.
The place of my comfort and rest,
Quiet and peace.

This is my working place.
The place of my dedication and strength,
Pride and honor.

This is my loving place.
The place of my family and heart,
Warmth and shelter.

This is my memory place.
The place of my seasons and sensations,
Traditions and transitions.

This is my hoping place.
The place of my dreams and desires,
Visions and wonder.

This is my mourning place.
The place of endings and beginnings,
Grief and renewal.

This is my dying place.
The place of my release and surrender,
Letting go and passing on.

This is my dwelling place.
The place of my moments and years,
Blessings and gifts,
Sabbaths of the heart,
Sabbaths of the soul.

Gather Me

Gather me unto my people,
The house of my ancestors,
The dwelling of our fathers and mothers,
The generations of our people.

This is my comfort,
Oh, my Rock,
This is my consolation,
Oh, my Redeemer,
That my bones will not be left behind,
That I will join the millennium,
And will reside in Your loving embrace,
In the abode of comfort and grace.

Gather me unto my people,
Unto my history,
Unto my legacy and my longing.

Let my heart and soul   הַנַּח לְלִבִּי וּלְנִשְׁמָתִי
Rest in peace.   לָנוּחַ בְּשָׁלוֹם.

*Hanach l'libi u'lnishmati
lanu'ach b'shalom.*

YIZKOR AND
MEMORIAL PRAYERS

In Memory of an Organ Donor

God of endings and beginnings,
God of past and future,
God of death and life,
Grant a perfect rest to _____ [insert name],
Whose death brought new life and new hope to others
Through the gift of his/her [vital] organs.
May those who received these gifts live lives of health and
    service,
Reflecting the love and devotion,
And the highest ideals,
Of [our/my] [father/mother/sister/brother/child/wife/dear one].
Bless our family with joy and peace that the hour of his/her
    death
Became a moment of life for others.
May this act of generosity echo through the generations,
A source of hope and comfort.
May his/her soul be bound up in the bond of life,
A living blessing in our midst.

For Donor Families

Ancient One,
God of healing,
Bless the family of _____ [insert name],
Of righteous memory,
Who was taken from their midst.
In the time of their deepest heartbreak
They had the strength and courage,
Generosity and kindness,
To choose life by donating her/his organs
For the benefit of others.
Bring wholeness and healing to his/her family.
May their strength resound through the generations.
May their love never cease.
Let their gift serve as a call to others
To follow this righteous path.

Grant Your blessings upon
All who are touched by transplant:
Donors, recipients and families,
Doctors and nurses,
Clinicians and administrators,
The vast network of professionals and volunteers
Who dedicate themselves to healing.

God of compassion,
May this gift of life
Become a source of consolation and comfort,
Holiness and grace.

For Those Who Donated Their
Bodies to Medical Research

God of endings and beginnings,
God of past and future,
God of life,
Grant a perfect rest to those who gave freely of themselves
    in death,
Donating their bodies to medical research,
Reflecting love and devotion for others
And the highest ideals of service to humankind.
Grant medical scientists the wisdom to use these gifts wisely,
So that their research will yield new knowledge and insight
Leading to new treatments and cures.
Bless donor families with peace,
Knowing that the hour of death
Became a source of hope and life for others.
May this act of generosity echo through the generations,
May their souls be bound up in the bond of life,
A living blessing in our midst.

Meditation on the Burial of a Young Child

My dear _____ [insert name],
My son/daughter/child,
Your hands were so small,
Your skin, so smooth,
Your smile, as bright as sunlight.
We had so little time,
And so much more to do, to discover, to share.

Oh, grief,
Oh, loneliness and sorrow,
The coffin that holds you is so small,
The wood, so smooth,
This moment, dark with despair.
And still, your laughter echoes in my heart,
And your face shines in my eyes.

[If desired, speak silently or aloud memories and moments to
    honor the life of your child and the difficult days ahead.]

God of compassion,
Grant our family the wisdom to be gentle with each other
In these hours of grievous loss.
Lead us on the path to hope and renewal,
So that we may become a well
Of comfort and support for each other.

God of All,
Grant a perfect rest among the souls of the righteous
To _____ [insert name],
My son/daughter/child who has gone to his/her eternal rest.
May his/her memory be sanctified with love and
May his/her soul be bound up in the bond of life,
A living blessing in our midst.

At the Hand of Violence: A Yizkor *Prayer*

Author of life
Source and Creator,
Grant a perfect rest under Your tabernacle of peace
To _____ [insert name],
My [father/mother/sister/brother/child/wife/dear one/friend],
Whose life was cut off by violence,
An act of witless aggression.
We remember his/her wisdom, talents and skills,
Joy, laughter and tears.
Let these memories continue to bless us
Even as we pray for him/her to find peace
In the world to come.
Put an end to anger, hatred and fear,
And lead us to a time when no one will suffer at the hand of
    another.
May his/her soul be bound up in the bond of life,
A living blessing in our midst.

After a Deadly Rampage

Author of life
Source and Creator,
Grant a perfect rest under Your tabernacle of peace
To the victims of the massacre
In _____ [insert place of the event],
Whose lives were cut off by violence,
A rampage of witless aggression beyond understanding.
Their hopes were severed.
Their dreams were lost to brutality.
May their souls be bound up in the bond of life,
A living blessing in our midst.
May they rest in peace.

God of justice and mercy,
Remember, too, the survivors of this attack,
Witnesses of shock, horror and dismay.
Ease their suffering and release their trauma,
So that they recover lives of joy and wonder.
Grant them Your shelter and solace,
Blessing and renewal.
Grant them endurance to survive,
Strength to rebuild,
Faith to mourn,
And courage to heal.
Remember the families and friends
Of the dead and the wounded.
With comfort and consolation.
Grant them Your protection,
Your wholeness and healing.
May they find hope and renewal.
Heavenly Guide,
Source of love and shelter,
Put an end to anger, hatred and fear,
And lead us to a time when
No one will suffer at the hand of another,
Speedily, in our day.

Yizkor *for a Soldier*

God of the selfless,
God of the strong and the brave,
Grant a perfect rest among the souls of the righteous
To _____ [insert name],
My [father/mother/sister/brother/child/wife/dear one/friend],
Who died in service to our country during the _____
    [insert name of war or conflict].
May his/her dedication serve as a shining lamp of courage
    and love.
Bless the souls of all who have died in the name of liberty
    and democracy,
Soldiers and veterans,
Civilians and professionals,
Men and women who answered the call of honor and duty.
May his/her memory be sanctified with joy and love.
May his/her soul be bound up in the bond of life,
A living blessing in our midst.

Yizkor *for First Responders*

God of the selfless,
God of the strong and the brave,
Grant a perfect rest among the souls of the righteous
To _____ [insert name],
My [father/mother/sister/brother/child/wife/dear one/friend/
    other relationship],
Who died in service to others [in/during/because of]
    _____ [insert name of event: the 9/11 attacks on
    the United States, the Mount Carmel forest fire or other
    event].
May his/her dedication to protecting life serve as a shining
    lamp of love
And the works of his/her hands bring us all merit in heaven.
Bless the souls of all who have died to save others,
Civilians and professionals,
The trained and the untrained,
In every age and in every land,
Men and women who answered the call of honor, duty and
    service.
May the memory of _____ [insert name]
Be sanctified with joy and love.
May his/her soul be bound up in the bond of life,
A living blessing in our midst.

REMEMBERING 9/11

For 9/11 Survivors

God of the survivor,
God of the mourner and the witness,
Grant solace and peace to those still held by physical,
    emotional and spiritual distress from the attacks of 9/11.
Release them from visions of death and destruction, from
    guilt or shame, from fear or anger.
Bind their wounds with Your steadfast love.
Lift them on Your wings of kindness and grace.

Blessed are those who have found peace.
    Blessed are those without tranquillity.
Blessed are those who speak.
    Blessed are those who stay silent.
Blessed are those who have healed.
    Blessed are those who suffer.
Blessed are those who forgive.
    Blessed are those who cannot forgive.

Blessed are You, *Adonai*	בָּרוּךְ אַתָּה ה' אֱלֹקֵינוּ,
our God,	מְקוֹר עָצְמָה לִשְׂרִידֵי אַלִּימוּת
Source of strength for	וּזְוָעָה בְּכָל מָקוֹם וּבְכָל זְמַן.
survivors of violence	בָּרוּךְ אַתָּה, צוּר יִשְׂרָאֵל,
and tragedy in every	מְקוֹר הַתִּקְוָה וְהַנֶּחָמָה.
land and in every age.	
Blessed are You, Rock	
of Israel,	
Source of hope and comfort.	

Baruch atah Adonai Eloheinu,
m'kor otzmah lisridei alimut u'zva'ah
b'chol makom u'vchol z'man.
Baruch atah, Tzur Yisrael, m'kor hatikvah v'hanechamah.

At the Hand of Terror: A 9/11 Yizkor *Prayer*

Creator of all,
Source and Shelter,
Grant a perfect rest under Your tabernacle of peace
To _____ [insert name(s)],
My [father/mother/sister/brother/child/wife/dear one/friend],
Who died [in/during/because of]
The 9/11 attacks on the United States.
Remember the works of his/her hands
And the message of his/her heart.
Remember all those who were lost in the terror of that day.
Grant their families peace and comfort for Your name's sake
And for the sake of those who perished.
Bring an end to violence and terror,
Speedily, in our days.
May the memory of _____ [insert name(s)]
Be sanctified with joy and love.
May his/her/their soul[s] be bound up in the bond of life,
A living blessing in our midst.

At the Hand of Terror II:
A 9/11 Memorial Prayer

Creator of all,
Source and Shelter,
Grant a perfect rest under Your tabernacle of peace
To those who died in the 9/11 attacks on the United States.
Remember the works of their hands
And the message of their hearts.
Grant their families peace and comfort for Your name's sake
And for the sake of those who perished.
Bring an end to violence and terror,
Speedily, in our days.
May their memories be sanctified with joy and love.
May their souls be bound up in the bond of life,
A living blessing in our midst.

Memorial Prayer for 9/11 First Responders

God of the selfless,
God of the strong and the brave,
Grant a perfect rest among the souls of the righteous
To those who died in service to others because of
The 9/11 attacks on the United States.
May their dedication to protecting life serve as a shining
     lamp of love
And the works of their hands bring us all merit in heaven.
Bless the souls of all who have died to save others,
Civilians and professionals,
The trained and the untrained,
In every age and in every land,
Men and women who answered the call of honor, duty and
     service.
May their memories be sanctified with joy and love.
May their souls be bound up in the bond of life,
A living blessing in our midst.

HOLOCAUST AND ANTI-SEMITISM

At the Hand of Anti-Semitism: A Yizkor *Prayer*

Creator of all,
Source and Shelter,
Grant a perfect rest under Your tabernacle of peace
To _____ [insert name(s)],
My [father/mother/sister/brother/child/wife/dear one/friend],
Whose life was [lives were] cut off by violence,
An act of witless aggression
And calculated anti-Semitism.
We remember his/her/their wisdom, talents and skills,
Joy, laughter and tears.
We remember the works of his/her/their hands
And the message of his/her/their heart[s].
Let these memories continue to bless us
Even as we pray for him/her/them to find peace
In the world to come.
Remember the virtues of those who have died
At the hand of malice
In every generation.
Bless the defenders of Israel
With safety and strength,
And the righteous of all nations who
Provide protection, shelter and comfort
To our people.
Put an end to anger, hatred and fear,
And lead us to a time when no one will suffer at the hand of
    another,
Speedily, in our days.
May the memory of _____ [insert name(s)]
Be sanctified with joy and love.
May his/her/their soul[s] be bound up in the bond of life,
A living blessing in our midst.

Shoah Memorial Prayer

Creator of all,
Source and Shelter,
Grant a perfect rest under Your tabernacle of peace
To those who perished in the Holocaust,
Our fathers and mothers,
Our sisters and brothers,
Our rabbis and teachers,
Our neighbors and children,
The named and the unnamed,
Whose lives were cut off by
Brutal, vicious, cunning, calculated violence.
May they find peace in the world to come.
Remember the survivors who have since passed away,
And the virtues of our people who have died at the hand of
    malice
In every generation.
We remember the works of their hands
And the messages of their hearts.
Bless the defenders of Israel with safety and strength
And the righteous of all nations who provide
Protection, shelter and comfort to the Jewish people.
Let their deeds be a source of favor in heaven
And healing on earth.
Put an end to anger, hatred and fear,
And lead us to a time when no one will suffer at the hand of
    another,
Speedily, in our days.
May the memories of all who faced these horrors
Be sanctified with joy and love.
May their souls be bound up in the bond of life,
A living blessing in our midst.

After the Horror

Hold fast to the breath of life.
Hold fast to the song of life.
Hold fast to the soul of life.

This is my sacred duty, God of old,
As survivor, as witness, as a voice of history and truth.
Why else did I live when so many died?
Why else do I stand when so many were put to rest?
Why else do I hope and yearn when so many were silenced?

Hold fast to awe and wonder.
Hold fast to radiance and light.
Hold fast to mystery and majesty.

This is my sacred duty, God of old,
As mourner, as testimony to horror and destruction.
What else remains? What else endures?
What more can You ask of me,
But to choose life in the shadow of death?

Tears of Crystal, Tears of Broken Glass

My tears are crystal and broken glass.
They sparkle, they cut.
They heal, they wound.
They are daybreak and midnight,
Hymn and dirge,
Joyous celebration and lonely mourning.
My tears catch Your Divine light,
Prisms casting colors across my days
And on my hands.
I pray to hold them gently,
With dignity,
With honor.

I am one of Your children,
One of those You love,
Comforted knowing that I, too,
Am one for whom You cry
Tears of crystal,
Tears of broken glass.

Munich Massacre Memorial Prayer

Creator of all,
Source and Shelter,
We remember as yesterday
The day of Olympic terror,
The day that our brothers,
Athletes and coaches,
Lost their lives to brutal violence,
And our hearts are melting with sorrow.
We remember their joy and their dreams,
Their enthusiasm and their hope,
Their spirit and their valor,
Their love for each other,
Their dedication to competition.
Grant them a perfect rest under Your tabernacle of peace.
Grant their families consolation and comfort
For Your name's sake
And for the sake of those who perished.

Ancient One,
Remember the virtues of all who have
Died at the hand of hatred.
May their memory become our resolve
To protect our land and our people.
Watch over the defenders of Israel.
Bless them with safety and strength.
May their courage never falter.
Grant Your protection and shelter to all who travel under
    the flag of Israel
In the name of cooperation, understanding and goodwill:
Athletes, musicians, performers, artists and scholars.
May their spirit be a shining light of integrity and honor.
Grant the whole house of Israel safety throughout the earth,
Free from aggression and violence.

God of old,
Shine a light of compassion into the world.
Put an end to malice, anger and fear.
Lead us to a time when no one will suffer at the hand of
another,
A time when our people can travel without the threat of
terror.
May the memories of those murdered
In the Munich massacre
Be sanctified with joy and love.
May their souls be bound up in the bond of life,
A living blessing in our midst.

HEALING THE BODY

GENERAL PRAYERS
FOR HEALING

Quick Prayer for Healing

God of love,
Cast the light of health and well-being
On the injured, the infirm and the insecure,
All who yearn for Your healing hand.
Bless them with healing of body,
Healing of soul,
And healing of spirit.
Grant all in need a full and complete recovery.

Blessed are You, *Adonai* our בָּרוּךְ אַתָּה ה׳ אֱלֹקֵינוּ, מְקוֹר חַיִּים.
    God, Source of life.

Baruch atah Adonai Eloheinu, m'kor chayim.

Quick Prayer for My Healing

God of love,
Cast the light of health and well-being on me [and on my
    family]
And all who are injured, infirm or insecure.
We yearn for Your healing hand.
Bless us with healing of body,
Healing of soul,
And healing of spirit.
Grant all in need a full and complete recovery.

Blessed are You, *Adonai* our   בָּרוּךְ אַתָּה ה' אֱלֹקֵינוּ, מְקוֹר חַיִּים.
    God, Source of life.

Baruch atah Adonai Eloheinu, m'kor chayim.

Quick Prayer for Healing (specific)

God of love,
Cast the light of health and well-being on
_____ [insert name],
[His/Her family]
And all who are injured, infirm or insecure,
Those who yearn for Your healing hand.
Bless them with healing of body,
Healing of soul
And healing of spirit.
Grant all in need a full and complete recovery.

Blessed are You, *Adonai* our   בָּרוּךְ אַתָּה ה' אֱלֹקֵינוּ, מְקוֹר חַיִּים.
    God, Source of life.

Baruch atah Adonai Eloheinu, m'kor chayim.

Inviting Healing

Radiance and awe,
Splendor and wonder,
The energy of being surrounds me,
Flowing day by day
From the holy realms.

Let me invite these gifts of holiness
Into my hands,
Into my body,
Into the core of my being.

Let me invite the energy of life
Into my limbs,
Into my chest,
Into my heart.

Let me invite this well of healing
Into my breath,
Into my blood,
Into my spirit.

God of old,
Healer and Guide,
You have blessed me with life,
Days of hope and yearning.
Bless me with Your healing power.
Lead me back to
A life of wholeness and peace.

This Well of Pain

This well of pain,
This terror inside me,
Seems to have no end.
It rises up from a place
Beyond this realm of flesh
To hold my body hostage,
To trouble my days
And to grieve my heart.

God of old,
Grant me the will to endure
And the strength to survive
The stream of suffering,
For You are the well of healing
And the river of life.
Grant me moments of relief
On the path to a full recovery.

Blessed are You, *Adonai*
   our God, Ruler of
   the universe,
Who gives strength
   to the weary.

בָּרוּךְ אַתָּה ה' אֱלֹקֵינוּ מֶלֶךְ הָעוֹלָם,
הַנּוֹתֵן לַיָּעֵף כֹּחַ.

Baruch atah Adonai Eloheinu melech ha'olam,
hanotein laya'eif ko'ach.

For Endurance

My body is a mystery,
So strong, so fragile.
It can suffer great pain,
Endure to reach triumph,
But a small moment can bring collapse and death.

My body is a mystery,
A gift of intricacy and beauty.
Powerful,
Endowed with the ability to take light and air and food
And turn them into energy and action.

What, then, is my life?
How, then, will I use this gift?

I will thank You for Your kindness and abundance.
I will treasure the moments of strength and vigor.
I will surrender to moments of weakness and distress.

God, who provides sustenance and health,
You are the Source of life.

Relief from Chronic Pain

God of mercy,
I have lived with chronic pain
For [years / as long as I can remember / what seems like
    forever],
Sometimes sharp, sometimes dull,
At times mild, at times intense,
Always present.
Grant me relief from this thief
That drains my energy,
Robbing my sleep,
Tormenting my days,
Fraying my nerves,
Attacking my sense of wholeness
And well-being.

God of compassion,
Help me to live a life of dignity and love,
Patience and serenity,
Kindness and grace,
In the shadow of this oppression,
In the shadow of this loss.

God of love,
Ease my suffering,
Reduce my burden,
Restore my health,
And grant me a life of
Joy and hope.

Blessed are You, *Adonai*   בָּרוּךְ אַתָּה ה' אֱלֹקֵינוּ מֶלֶךְ הָעוֹלָם,
    our God, Ruler of   הַנּוֹתֵן לַיָּעֵף כֹּחַ.
    the universe,
Who gives strength
    to the weary.

Baruch atah Adonai Eloheinu melech ha'olam,
hanotein laya'eif ko'ach.

Relief of a Loved One's Chronic Pain

God of mercy,
My [father/mother/brother/sister/husband/wife/spouse/
   partner/friend]
Lives with chronic pain,
Day in and day out,
Draining his/her energy,
Robbing his/her sleep,
Tormenting his/her days,
Fraying his/her nerves,
Attacking his/her sense of wholeness
And well-being.

God of compassion,
Grant him/her relief.
Help him/her to live a life of dignity and love,
Patience and serenity,
Kindness and grace,
In the shadow of this oppression,
In the shadow of this loss.

God of love,
Ease this suffering,
Reduce this burden,
Restore his/her health
And grant him/her a life of
Joy and hope.

Blessed are You, *Adonai*   בָּרוּךְ אַתָּה ה' אֱלֹקֵינוּ מֶלֶךְ הָעוֹלָם,
   our God, Ruler of   הַנּוֹתֵן לַיָּעֵף כֹּחַ.
   the universe,
Who gives strength
   to the weary.

Baruch atah Adonai Eloheinu melech ha'olam,
hanotein laya'eif ko'ach.

On Recurrent Pain

God of old,
My pain has diminished,
The trouble has eased,
This grief has, for now, faded.
Thank You for these moments of relief
After the hours of affliction,
These moments of quiet inside me,
These times of rest.
Thank You for those who have
Dedicated themselves to my care.
Thank You for the chance to regain
A sense of wholeness,
A sense of calm,
A sense of peace.

Ancient One,
Well of healing,
Grant healing power to my physicians
And my medications.
Grant comfort and healing to all who suffer.
Grant me the strength to endure
When the pain returns.

Blessed are You, *Adonai*   בָּרוּךְ אַתָּה ה' אֱלֹקֵינוּ מֶלֶךְ הָעוֹלָם,
  our God, Ruler of   הַנּוֹתֵן לַיָּעֵף כֹּחַ.
  the universe,
Who gives strength
  to the weary.

Baruch atah Adonai Eloheinu melech ha'olam,
hanotein laya'eif ko'ach.

SURGERY

Before My Surgery

God of health and healing,
I surrender myself to the physician's skill,
The surgeon's gift,
The nurse's care,
Placing my body in the cradle of others,
Just as I place my soul in Your loving arms.

Bless my surgeon with a steady hand,
Keen vision,
And a passion for healing.

Bless my caregivers with wisdom and skill,
With compassion, focus and dedication.

Bless my family with ease and comfort.
Give them energy and endurance, tranquillity and peace.
Remind them to care for themselves and each other,
Even as their hearts and prayers turn to me.

Bless my body with strength,
My spirit with courage,
My thoughts with hope,
And my life with renewed purpose.

Source of life,
Bless us with Your guidance,
Make us Your partner in healing,
And grant a full and speedy recovery.

Before a Loved One's Surgery

God of health and healing,
Watch over my [father/mother/brother/sister/husband/wife/
    spouse/partner/friend]
As he/she faces [major/lifesaving/emergency] surgery.
Bless his/her surgeon with a steady hand,
Keen vision and a passion for healing,
Just as I pray for You to hold his/her soul gently and with
    love.
Bless his/her caregivers with focus and compassion,
With wisdom and dedication.
Bless our family with ease and comfort,
Energy and endurance, tranquillity and strength.

Source of life,
Bring Your healing power to _____ [insert name].
Remove her/his pain,
Relieve her/his distress,
And restore her/his body, mind and spirit,
Renewing her/him to wholeness and peace.
Bless her/him with vigor, courage and hope,
So that she/he may know life and health,
Joy and love.
And grant her/him a full and speedy recovery.

Blessed are You, God   בָּרוּךְ אַתָּה, הָאֵל הַנִּסְתָּר,
    of mystery,   מְקוֹר הַבְּרִיאוּת וְהָרְפּוּי.
Source of health and healing.

Baruch atah, ha'El hanistar,
m'kor hab'ri'ut v'haripuy.

Before My Child's Surgery

God of health and healing,
I surrender my daughter/son to the physician's skill,
The surgeon's gift,
The nurse's care,
Placing her/his body into the cradle of others,
Just as I pray for You to hold her/his soul gently and with
    love.
Watch over my daughter/son throughout this journey.
Bless her/his surgeon with a steady hand,
Keen vision and a passion for healing.
Bless her/his caregivers with focus and compassion,
With wisdom and dedication.
Grant my [husband/wife/partner/spouse] and me patience
    and fortitude
During these hours of uncertainty
And the ability to make sound judgments in this hour of need.
Bless our entire family with ease and comfort,
Energy and endurance, tranquillity and strength.

Source of life,
Bring Your healing power to _____ [insert name].
Remove her/his pain,
Relieve her/his distress,
And restore her/his body, mind and spirit,
Renewing her/him to wholeness and peace.
Bless her/him with vigor, courage and hope,
So that she/he may know life and health,
Joy and love.
And grant her/him a full and speedy recovery.

Blessed are You, God   בָּרוּךְ אַתָּה, הָאֵל הַנִּסְתָּר,
    of mystery,   מְקוֹר הַבְּרִיאוּת וְהָרִפּוּי.
Source of health and healing.

Baruch atah, ha'El hanistar,
m'kor hab'ri'ut v'haripuy.

After My Surgery

God of renewal and strength,
Thank You for seeing me
Through the many traumas of surgery.
Bless my body with the gifts of vitality and renewal
As I move through the process of recovery.
Grant me rest, comfort and healing.
Bless my body and spirit with Your Divine energy,
Endowed by Your loving hand,
On the path to wholeness.

Bless all of us whose recovery is not yet complete,
All whose future remains uncertain.
Erase our worries,
Console our children,
Strengthen our parents,
Fortify our partners
And bring peace to our families and friends.

May the One who heals   מִי יִתֵּן כִּי הַמְרַפֵּא בִּקְדֻשָׁה וּבְאַהֲבָה
   with holiness and love   יַעֲנִיק הַחְלָמָה לְכָל נִזְקָק.
Grant recovery to all in need.

Mi yitein ki ham'rapei bikdushah uv'ahavah
ya'anik hachlamah l'chol nizkak.

After a Loved One's Surgery

God of renewal and strength,
Thank You for seeing my [father/mother/brother/sister/
    husband/wife/spouse/partner/friend]
Through the many traumas of surgery.
Bless him/her with the gifts of vitality,
Comfort and recovery,
Continued health and healing,
As his/her body and spirit use Your Divine energy,
Endowed by Your loving hand,
To find wholeness.

Bless those whose recovery is not yet complete,
Whose future remains uncertain.
Erase their worries,
Console their children,
Strengthen their parents,
Fortify their partners,
And bring peace to their families and friends.

May the One who heals   מִי יִתֵּן כִּי הַמְרַפֵּא בִּקְדֻשָּׁה וּבְאַהֲבָה
    with holiness and love   יַעֲנִיק הַחְלָמָה לְכָל נִזְקָק.
Grant recovery to all in need.

Mi yitein ki ham'rapei bikdushah uv'ahavah
ya'anik hachlamah l'chol nizkak.

After My Child's Surgery

God of renewal and strength,
Thank You for seeing [my/our] [son/daughter]
Through the many traumas of surgery.
Bless him/her with the gifts of comfort,
Healing and recovery,
As his/her body and spirit use Your Divine energy,
Endowed by Your loving hand,
On the journey toward wholeness.

Ease his/her pain.
Remove his/her suffering.
Grant him/her courage and endurance throughout these
    challenges,
Moments of joy and humor,
Happiness and love.

Bless [my/our][son/daughter]
And all children whose recovery is not yet complete.
Erase their worries,
Strengthen their parents,
Fortify their partners
And bring peace to their families and friends.

May the One who heals   מִי יִתֵּן כִּי הַמְרַפֵּא בִּקְדֻשָׁה וּבְאַהֲבָה
    with holiness and love   יַעֲנִיק הַחְלָמָה לְכָל נִזְקָק.
Grant recovery to all in need.

*Mi yitein ki ham'rapei bikdushah uv'ahavah
ya'anik hachlamah l'chol nizkak.*

Upon My Recovery from Surgery

God of renewal and strength,
Thank You for the gifts of vitality, comfort and recovery
After the many traumas of surgery.

Grant me continued health and healing
As my body and spirit use Your Divine energy,
Endowed by Your loving hand,
To find wholeness.

Bless my surgeon with skill and my caregivers with love,
So that others may know the awesome wonder
Of new spirit,
New joy,
And renewed life.

Bless those whose recovery is not yet complete,
Whose future remains uncertain.
Erase their worries,
Console their children,
Strengthen their parents,
Fortify their partners,
And bring peace to their families and friends.

May the One who heals	מִי יִתֵּן כִּי הַמְרַפֵּא בִּקְדֻשָּׁה וּבְאַהֲבָה
with holiness and love	יַעֲנִיק הַחְלָמָה לְכָל נִזְקָק.
Grant recovery to all in need.	

*Mi yitein ki ham'rapei bikdushah uv'ahavah
ya'anik hachlamah l'chol nizkak.*

PREGNANCY
AND FERTILITY

For Pregnancy

God of our mothers,
My yearning is as old as creation,
As old as love,
As old as life.

Bless my body with the wonders of pregnancy
And my days with the promise of birth.
Bless my heart with the gift of a child
And my soul with the gift of hope,
The gift of generations.

God of mercy,
My yearning is as fresh as dew,
Ripe with longing,
Ripe with desire.
Hear my voice.
[Hear my grief.]
Hear my prayer.

Blessed are You, Source of life.   בָּרוּךְ אַתָּה, מְקוֹר חַיִּים.

Baruch atah, m'kor chayim.

For Fertility Treatment (women)

God of mercy,
I have prayed,
I have cried,
I have shown my sorrow to heaven,
In the name of fulfilling Your command,
In the name of fulfilling my birthright.
Mother.
Vessel of life.
Vessel of love.
Source of joy.
Source of generations.

Rock of Ages,
Has my body betrayed me?
Are my hopes and dreams
Empty, barren, lost?
Grant me courage and fortitude
As I begin/continue fertility treatments.
Grant my doctors wisdom
And my body strength,
So that I may know the holiness and wonder,
The radiance and light,
Of carrying life and giving birth,
In the fullness of health,
In the fullness of joy,
With awe and thanksgiving,
With gratitude and humility,
In service to Your Holy Name.

Blessed are You, Source of life.   בָּרוּךְ אַתָּה, מְקוֹר חַיִּים.

Baruch atah, m'kor chayim.

For Fertility Treatment (men)

God of our fathers,
God of generations,
How strange is this feeling?
How odd to hear that
My body and my seed are weak,
That I need medical help to fulfill my duty,
My honor, my joy,
Of partnership in creating a child.

Rock of Ages,
Grant me courage and fortitude
As I begin/continue fertility treatments.
Grant my doctors wisdom
And my body strength,
So that I may know the wonder of fatherhood,
The holiness, radiance and light
Of bringing life.
Grant me/us a child
In the fullness of health,
In the fullness of joy,
With awe and thanksgiving,
With gratitude and humility,
In service to Your Holy Name.

Blessed are You, Source of life.   .בָּרוּךְ אַתָּה, מְקוֹר חַיִּים

Baruch atah, m'kor chayim.

Waiting for Fertility Test Results

Ancient One,
God of hope,
This moment is familiar,
And this moment is new.
This waiting. This hoping. This praying.
What will the news bring?
What decisions will I face?
How will I cope in the days ahead?
Bless me with the gift of a child,
With the gift of generations,
With the gift of love.

God of old,
Grant me the wisdom to be gentle with myself
In these hours of uncertainty.
Bless me with courage and wisdom,
With patience and understanding.
Show me the grace and insight to use this time as a moment
    of rest,
Perhaps to find a well of gratitude
For the gifts You have already given.
Surround me with Your warmth.
Cradle me in Your care.

Blessed are You, Source of life.   בָּרוּךְ אַתָּה, מְקוֹר חַיִּים.

Baruch atah, m'kor chayim.

To a Spouse/Partner during Fertility Treatments

My darling,
Dear _____ [insert name],
Our journey has been long
In the name of joy,
In the name of creating a family,
In the name of becoming parents.
We have prayed,
We have cried,
And we have shown our sorrow to heaven.

God of compassion,
Grant us the wisdom to be gentle with ourselves
And with each other
In these hours of [sorrow and] hope,
In these days of [fear and] uncertainty.
Show us the path to gratitude,
For the gift of our lives
And our seasons together,
So that we may become a well
Of comfort and support for each other.

God of creation,
Mother of life,
Father of the universe,
Bless us with the gift of a child,
With the gift of generations,
With the gift of love.

Blessed are You, Source of life.   בָּרוּךְ אַתָּה, מְקוֹר חַיִּים.

Baruch atah, m'kor chayim.

When a High-Risk Pregnancy Is Confirmed (women)

Source of life,
With joy and celebration,
With hope and gratitude,
With care and caution,
Knowing the risks and challenges ahead,
I/We pause to give thanks
For this pregnancy,
This potential for new life.

Grant my doctors wisdom
And my body strength,
So that I may know the holiness and wonder,
The radiance and light,
Of carrying life and giving birth,
And the joy of motherhood.

God of love,
Grant [me/us] [this child/these children]
In the fullness of health,
In the fullness of joy,
The gift of generations,
A gift of glory beyond measure.

Blessed are You, Source of life.   .בָּרוּךְ אַתָּה, מְקוֹר חַיִּים

Baruch atah, m'kor chayim.

When a High-Risk Pregnancy Is Confirmed (men/partners)

Source of life,
With joy and celebration,
With hope and gratitude,
With care and caution,
Knowing the risks and challenges ahead,
I/We pause to give thanks
For this pregnancy,
This potential for new life.

Grant our doctors wisdom
And my wife/partner strength,
So that I may know
The holiness, radiance and light,
Of bringing life,
And the joy and wonder of [fatherhood/parenthood].

God of love,
Grant [me/us] [this child/these children]
In the fullness of health,
In the fullness of joy,
The gift of generations,
A gift of glory beyond measure.

Blessed are You, Source of life.   בָּרוּךְ אַתָּה, מְקוֹר חַיִּים.

Baruch atah, m'kor chayim.

Loss of a Pregnancy (women)

God of old,
This pain has no breath,
This pain has no light,
This pain has no bottom,
An emptiness in the core of my being.
My heart, my breath, my womb,
Once full, once vital,
Once pulsing in service to creation,
Are vacant and hollow,
And I have touched a new sorrow,
A new loneliness,
A new grief.

[Rock of Ages,
Why have You raised my hope only to take it away?
Why have You forsaken my prayers and my dreams?
What comfort remains?]

Source and Shelter,
See me through the hours and days ahead with compassion
    and grace.
Help me to treat myself [and my husband/partner/spouse]
With kindness, patience and understanding.
Lead me out of this darkness,
Back to awe and wonder,
So I may know,
Once again,
Hope and joy,
Gratitude and peace.

Loss of a Pregnancy (men/partners)

God of old,
What can I say before You?
I am crushed,
Flattened by sadness,
Cut down by grief.
Yet my wife/partner/spouse needs
My courage and my tears,
My gentleness and my strength.
Our lives,
Once ripe with promise,
Feel vacant and hollow,
And I have touched
A new loneliness and despair.

[Rock of Ages,
Why have You raised our hopes only to take them away?
Why have You forsaken our prayers and our dreams?
What comfort remains?]

Source and Shelter,
Teach me to honor, to balance and to express
Both my pain and my fortitude,
My endurance and my sorrow,
In service to You,
In service to my wife/partner,
In service to myself.
Lead me/us out of this darkness,
Back to awe and wonder,
So I/we may know,
Once again,
Hope and joy,
Gratitude and peace.

CANCER

Cancer Fear

God of old,
I am overwhelmed with fear,
Devoured by terror,
At the news that [I may have cancer / my cancer may have
    returned].
This dread in my chest,
In my throat, in my heart and in my eyes,
Fills the core of my being
With a hungry panic,
Consuming my security,
Consuming my peace of mind.

God of health and healing,
Release me from worry and alarm
As I seek answers to challenging questions,
[Unbelievable questions,]
Unwanted questions.

Gracious One,
Grant me strength in these hours of uncertainty.
Grant me serenity as I wait for news.
Release my family and friends from worry
And make me an example of dignity and courage,
Even as I live in the shadow of the unknown.

Compassionate One,
Let health and healing surround me.
Let health and healing surround all of Your children.

Cancer Fear, Family or Friend

God of old,
My [father/mother/sister/brother/child/wife/husband/
    partner/dear one/friend] is overwhelmed with fear,
Devoured by terror,
At the news that [he/she may have cancer][his/her cancer
    may have returned].
He/she is trapped in the grip of dread,
A hungry panic, consuming his/her security,
Consuming his/her peace of mind.
And I, too, struggle with the possibilities.

God of health and healing,
Release us from worry and alarm
As we wait for answers to challenging questions,
[Unbelievable questions,]
Unwanted questions.

Gracious One,
Grant us strength in these hours of uncertainty.
Grant us serenity as we wait for news.
Release us from worry
As we live in the shadow of the unknown.

Compassionate One,
Let health and healing surround us.
Let health and healing surround all of Your children.

Waiting for a Pre-Diagnosis Biopsy and Results

God of health and healing,
Source of my life,
Has my body turned against me?
Have my cells become agents of disease?

God of my ancestors,
God of hope,
Grant me strength as I wait for [my biopsy / the results of
    my biopsy]
With dignity and resolve,
With [confusion/sorrow/anger/fear/doubt][and]
    [_____ (insert words that describe your feelings)].
Stand with me as I await news and, if necessary,
Grant me the clarity to make sound choices
For my treatment and my life.
Grant my family comfort and relief
In this time of uncertainty.

Ancient One,
God of old,
Provide my physicians knowledge and insight.
Give scientists and researchers tools and understanding
To develop new treatments for all forms of cancer,
Speedily, in our day.
Grant me courage.
Set my life on a path to wholeness and well-being.

Waiting for a Follow-Up Biopsy and Results

God of health and healing,
Source of my life,
I [will surrender / have surrendered] myself, again,
To the hands of my doctors
To check my body for disease.
[Has my treatment been effective?]
[Has my cancer spread?]
[Will the news bring hope?]
[Will the news bring new challenges?]

God of my ancestors,
Grant me strength as I wait for [my biopsy / the results of
    my biopsy]
With dignity and resolve,
With [confusion/sorrow/anger/fear/doubt][and]
    [_____ (insert words that describe your feelings)].
Stand with me as I await the news and, if necessary,
Grant me the clarity to make sound choices
For my treatment and my life.
Grant my family comfort and relief
In this time of uncertainty.

Ancient One,
God of old,
Provide my physicians knowledge and insight.
Give scientists and researchers tools and understanding
To develop new treatments for all forms of cancer,
Speedily, in our day.
Grant me courage.
Set my life on a path to wholeness and well-being.

Upon Receiving a Cancer Diagnosis

God of health and healing,
Source of my life,
My body has turned against me,
My cells have become agents of disease,
Attacking and invading my [organs/blood/skin/bones][and]
[_____ (insert any other description of the area
of disease, as appropriate)].

God of my ancestors,
Grant me the strength to face my [confusion/sorrow/anger/
fear/doubt][and][_____ (insert words that
describe your feelings)]
With dignity and hope.
Grant me the clarity to make sound choices
For my treatment and my life.
[Stand with me as I contend with pain and suffering
On a journey toward wholeness and healing.]
Grant my family comfort and relief.
Ease their burdens and ease their minds.
Grant my physicians knowledge and insight
And my caregivers skill and perseverance.
Grant scientists and researchers tools and understanding
To develop new treatments for this cancer,
Speedily, in our day.
Grant me a path to healing and recovery.

Ancient One,   מֵאָז וּמֵעוֹלָם,
God of old,   קֵל כָּל הַזְּמַנִּים,
You are my Rock and   אַתָּה צוּרִי וְגוֹאֲלִי.
    Redeemer.

Mei'az u'mei'olam,
El kol haz'manim,
atah tzuri v'go'ali.

Upon a Loved One's
Receiving a Cancer Diagnosis

God of health and healing,
Source of my life,
Cancer has entered my circle of family and friends [again].
It has touched my [wife/husband/partner/dear friend/
    companion],
_____ [insert name].
I am [angry/sad/amazed/dazed/confused][and][shocked/
    _____ (insert words that best describe your
    feelings)] by this news.

God of old,
Let his/her treatment go swiftly and easily,
Without complication.
Restore his/her health.
Return his/her vitality.
Provide the best doctors,
Dedicated nurses,
And compassionate caregivers.
Grant me strength,
And let me feel the love and support of our family and
    friends.

God of generations,
This journey will have its own rhythm,
Beyond anyone's control.
The course may be uneven and uncertain.
Grant him/her a path to healing and recovery.

Ancient One,   מֵאָז וּמֵעוֹלָם,
God of old,   קֵל כָּל הַזְּמַנִּים,
You are my Rock and   אַתָּה צוּרִי וְגוֹאֲלִי.
    Redeemer.

Mei'az u'mei'olam,
El kol haz'manim,
atah tzuri v'go'ali.

For Cancer Treatment

Today is the day,
God of old,
That I [begin to receive / begin another cycle of]
Treatment for my cancer,
This disease,
This intruder,
This malaise that has invaded my body and my life.

Grant healing power to the [surgery][radiation][and]
    [chemotherapy]
To which I surrender myself with [courage/fear/hope/
    strength][and][_____ (insert words that best
    describe your feelings)].
Reduce the side effects and eliminate any complications
    from this procedure,
And grant me a full and complete recovery from this disease.
Grant me the clarity to make sound choices for my
    treatment and my life.
Grant my family comfort and relief.
Ease their burdens and ease their minds.
Grant my physicians insight and perseverance.
Grant my caregivers knowledge and skill.
Grant scientists and researchers tools and understanding
To develop new treatments for this cancer,
Speedily, in our day.

God of compassion,
Grant me a path to healing.
See me through this day and the days ahead with dignity.
Strengthen my resolve to live fully and to love deeply.

Blessed are You, God of   בָּרוּךְ אַתָּה, קֵל הַבְּרִיאוּת וְהָרְפוּי.
    health and healing.

Baruch atah, El hab'ri'ut v'haripuy.

For a Loved One's Cancer Treatment

Today is the day,
God of old,
That my [wife/husband/partner/dear friend/companion],
_____ [insert name],
[Begins to receive / Begins another cycle of]
Treatment for cancer,
This disease,
This intruder,
That has invaded his/her body and our lives.

God of compassion,
Grant him/her a path to healing.
See him/her through this day and the days ahead with
     dignity.
Strengthen our resolve to live fully and to love deeply.

Grant healing power to his/her [surgery][radiation][and]
     [chemotherapy].
Reduce the side effects and eliminate any complications
     from this procedure
And grant him/her a full and complete recovery from this
     disease.
Grant his/her physicians insight and perseverance
And his/her caregivers knowledge and skill.
Grant scientists and researchers tools and understanding
To develop new treatments for this cancer,
Speedily, in our day.

God of mercy,
Give me the poise and clarity
To provide steadfast support on this journey,
With love and respect,
With kindness and compassion.
Grant our family comfort and relief.
Ease our burdens and ease our minds.

Blessed are You, God of
   health and healing.

בָּרוּךְ אַתָּה, קֵל הַבְּרִיאוּת וְהָרִפּוּי.

Baruch atah, El hab'ri'ut v'haripuy.

My Child's Cancer Diagnosis

Holy One,
Source of All Being,
My child,
My baby,
This gift from heaven,
Who brings joy and light into my life,
Has been diagnosed with cancer.

What struggles will she/he face?
What trials await?
Only You know.
Help her/him in these hours of need.
Help me in the days and weeks ahead.

God of compassion,
Bring Your healing power to my daughter/son
_____ [insert name],
So that she/he may know life and health,
Joy and love,
On a journey toward wholeness and healing.

Grant our family comfort and relief,
Our physicians knowledge and insight,
And our caregivers skill and perseverance.
[Give me the gentleness, awareness and presence of mind
     to care for my husband/wife/partner as we struggle
     together.]
[Grant me/us the skills and resources to help my/our other
     children as they struggle through this family trauma.]
Give me/us the strength to ask others to care for [me/us] in
     [my/our] pain and distress.
And grant scientists and researchers tools and understanding
To develop new treatments for this cancer,
Speedily, in our day.

Ancient One,
Stand with me/us.

God of old,   קֵל כָּל הַזְּמַנִּים,
You are my/our Rock   אַתָּה צוּרִי וְגוֹאֲלִי.
   and Redeemer.

       El kol haz'manim,
       atah tzuri v'go'ali.

My Child's Cancer Treatment

God of old,
My child, my baby,
[His/Her small body,]
Must now endure the hardships of cancer treatment.

This is my prayer:
Grant healing power to the [surgery][radiation][and]
    [chemotherapy]
That he/she faces.
May it be of maximum service on his/her journey to
    recovery.
Reduce the side effects and eliminate any complications
    from this procedure.
Ease his/her pain and answer his/her fears with Your abiding
    love.
Grant our family comfort and relief,
Our physicians knowledge and insight
And our caregivers skill and perseverance.
Grant scientists and researchers tools and understanding
To develop new treatments for this cancer,
Speedily, in our day.

God of compassion,
Grant my son/daughter
_____ [insert name]
A path to wholeness and healing.
See us through this day and the days ahead with dignity.
Strengthen our resolve to live fully and to love deeply.

Blessed are You, God of   בָּרוּךְ אַתָּה, קֵל הַבְּרִיאוּת וְהָרִפּוּי.
    health and healing.

Baruch atah, El hab'ri'ut v'haripuy.

My Cancer, My Children

My God,
In the days ahead,
The weeks and the months,
I will face challenges as I fight my cancer.
My heart and my hopes,
My love and my questions,
Also turn toward my children.
What will they learn?
What beliefs will they take in?
How will their experience of my disease
Shape their lives?

This I pray:
Let me be a source of love,
A light of comfort,
A lamp of hope,
A well of blessings.
Grant me the ability to care for my children,
Even as they yearn to provide support and understanding
    for me.

[Optional insert: Repeat the following paragraph for each
    child]
Bless my child _____ [insert name],
Who _____ [insert thoughts about what he/she is
    feeling now]
With _____ [insert specific concerns and prayers for
    that child].

God of health and healing,
Watch over my children
In their hour of need.
Let our love for each other
Shine brightly through the days ahead,
A testimony to Your Holy Name.

Cancer Remission

God of blessing,
God of wholeness,
My cancer treatment has been successful,
And my disease is now in remission.
The battle has been long and arduous.
The fight has taken its toll.
I have faced many traumas in this struggle.
I have received many gifts.

As my body and spirit begin to grow stronger,
I turn my energy toward spiritual and emotional renewal.
Thank You for the knowledge, insight and perseverance
Of my physicians, nurses and caregivers
As they worked toward my healing and recovery.
Thank You for the steadfast support of my family and
    friends.
Thank You for the gift of recovery.

God of life,
Grant me strength.
Keep me free of this and any cancer.
Protect my soul and my spirit.
Grant scientists and researchers tools and understanding
To develop new treatments for this disease,
Speedily, in our days.

Blessed are You,	בָּרוּךְ אַתָּה,
God of gifts and blessings,	קֵל הַמַּתָּנוֹת וְהַבְּרָכוֹת,
God of health and healing,	קֵל הַבְּרִיאוּת וְהָרְפוּי,
Source of life and love.	מְקוֹר חַיִּים וְאַהֲבָה.

Baruch atah,
El hamatanot v'hab'rachot,
El hab'ri'ut v'haripuy,
m'kor chayim v'ahavah.

Cancer Anniversary

God of health and healing,
As I approach the [first, second . . .]
Anniversary of successful cancer treatment,
My anxiety and [insert your other emotions: fear, anger,
    grief] have returned.
I also have a wondrous and surprising sense of optimism
    and hope.

I remember clearly the shock and trauma of my diagnosis.
The concern of family and friends.
The fear.
The sleepless nights.
The sadness and tears.
The moments of hope.
The moments when hope seemed lost.
I remember those who have succumbed to this disease.
And I am aware of the fragility of life.

Thank You, God on high,
For the past year[s] of health,
This time with my cancer in remission.
Thank You for the gifts and blessings in my life,
The diligence of my physicians,
The support of those around me,
And the hope of tomorrow.
May vigor and vitality accompany me always.

Blessed are You,   בָּרוּךְ אַתָּה,
God of our fathers   קֵל אֲבוֹתֵינוּ וְאִמּוֹתֵינוּ,
    and mothers,   קֵל הַמַּתָּנוֹת וְהַבְּרָכוֹת,
God of gifts and blessings,   מְקוֹר חַיִּים.
Source of life.

Baruch atah,
El avoteinu v'imoteinu,
El hamatanot v'hab'rachot,
m'kor chayim.

On the Recurrence of Cancer

God of old,
Source of my life,
I am crushed and shattered
By the recurrence of cancer.
My body has turned against me once more.
My cells have transformed, again, into agents of disease.

God of wisdom and strength,
Have I lived in the illusion of false hopes?
Have I lived, unknowingly, in the shadow of borrowed time?
Have I been betrayed by my body?
By medical science?
By my will to live?

God of my ancestors,
God of health and hope,
Hear this prayer as I attempt to comprehend this moment,
As I contend with the potential for renewed pain and
        distress
On a journey toward wholeness and healing.
Grant me the clarity to make sound choices
For my treatment and my life.
Grant my physicians knowledge and insight
And my caregivers skill and perseverance.
Grant scientists and researchers tools and understanding
To develop new treatments for this cancer,
Speedily, in our day.
Grant me dignity in the face of suffering and affliction.
Grant my family comfort and relief.
Relieve their burdens.
Ease their minds.
Grant me a path to healing and recovery.

Ancient One,   מֵאָז וּמֵעוֹלָם,
God of old,   קֵל כָּל הַזְּמַנִּים,
You are my Rock and   אַתָּה צוּרִי וְגוֹאֲלִי.
    Redeemer.

Mei'az u'mei'olam,
El kol haz'manim,
atah tzuri v'go'ali.

CRITICAL ILLNESS

For a Critically Ill Child

God who made all things,
Source of blessing and healing,
Well of mystery and love,
I [understand that / don't understand why]
Children face the same perils as adults.
I [accept that / don't accept that]
This is my son's/daughter's journey.
I [surrender / refuse to surrender]
My desires to Your will.
[Still, I pray.]

You who healed Miriam in the desert,
Bring Your healing power to my son/daughter
_____ [insert name],
So that he/she may know life and health,
Joy and love.

Bless all who face _____ [insert name of disease/
    condition afflicting child].
Give them wholeness and peace.
Provide wisdom and insight to scientists and researchers,
So that treatments and cures can be found for this
And all afflictions suffered by children,
Speedily in our days.

Grant our family and her/his caregivers fortitude and
compassion.
[Grant me/us the skills and resources to help my/our other
children as they struggle through this family trauma.]
[Give me the gentleness, awareness and presence of mind
to care for my husband/wife/partner as we struggle
together.]
And give me/us the strength to ask others to care for [me/us]
in [my/our] pain and distress.

God of our people,
Ancient Source of majesty,
Bring healing to all in need,
Grant relief to all who suffer,
And look with favor on my son/daughter _____
[insert name].

In this hour of uncertainty.
Bless him/her with strength,
Remove his/her pain,
Relieve his/her distress,
And cure his/her body, mind and spirit.

Blessed are You, God of mystery,
May health and healing come speedily to those in need.

For a Critically Ill Father

Holy One,
God of health and healing,
My father's body is failing.
Illness holds him.
Grief and fear hold me.

Ancient One,
Well of hope,
Grant my father
A quick and complete recovery.
Relieve his suffering.
Remove his pain.
Return him to health.
Restore him to life.

Rock of my heart,
Comfort and shelter,
You know the path ahead.
You know the journey.
You hear our prayers.
God who healed Miriam in the desert,
Bring Your healing power to my father,
_____ [insert name],
So that he may know life and health,
Joy and peace.

Blessed are You,
Adonai our God,
Creator of fatherly wisdom
     and strength,
Source of love,
Rock of life.

בָּרוּךְ אַתָּה ה' אֱלֹקֵינוּ,
בּוֹרֵא חָכְמָה וְכֹחַ אֲבָהִי,
מְקוֹר הָאַהֲבָה,
צוּר הַחַיִּים.

Baruch atah Adonai Eloheinu,
borei chochmah v'cho'ach avahi,
m'kor ha'ahavah,
tzur hachayim.

For a Critically Ill Mother

Holy One,
God of health and healing,
My mother's body is failing.
Illness holds her.
Grief and fear hold me.

Ancient One,
Well of hope,
Grant my mother
A quick and complete recovery.
Relieve her suffering.
Remove her pain.
Return her to health.
Restore her to life.

Rock of my heart,
Comfort and shelter,
You know the path ahead.
You know the journey.
You hear our prayers.
God who healed Miriam in the desert,
Bring Your healing power to my mother,
_____ [insert name],
So that she may know life and health,
Joy and peace.

Blessed are You,   בָּרוּךְ אַתָּה ה׳ אֱלֹקֵינוּ,
Adonai our God,   בּוֹרֵא חָכְמָה וְחֶסֶד אִמָּהִי,
Creator of motherly   צוּר הַחַיִּים,
    wisdom and grace,   מְקוֹר הָאַהֲבָה.
Rock of life,
Source of love.

Baruch atah Adonai Eloheinu,
borei chochmah v'chesed imahi,
tzur hachayim,
m'kor ha'ahavah.

My Illness, My Children

My God,
In the days ahead,
The weeks and the months,
I will face challenges as the result of _____ [insert
    type of surgery or the name of the disease].
My heart and my hopes,
My love and my questions,
Also turn toward my children.
How will their experience of my surgery/illness/condition
Shape their lives?
What will they learn?
What beliefs will they take in?

Grant me the ability to care for my children,
Even as they yearn to provide support and understanding
    for me.
Let me be a source of love,
A light of comfort,
A lamp of hope,
A well of blessings.

[Optional insert: Repeat the following paragraph for each
    child]
Bless my child _____ [insert name],
Who _____ [insert thoughts about what he/she is
    feeling now]
With _____ [insert specific concerns and prayers for
    that child].

God of health and healing,
Watch over my children
In their hour of need.
Let our love for each other
Shine brightly through the days ahead,
A testimony to Your Holy Name.

Waiting for an Organ Transplant

Ancient One,
Breath of life,
In Your wisdom You have given medical science
The skill and ability to transplant organs,
Renewing life for the critically ill.

God of compassion and mercy,
Bless [me] [my father/mother/sister/brother/child/wife/
    husband/partner/dear one/friend], _____ [insert
    name],
With this gift of life.
Release me/him/her from fear and pain,
From moments of uncertainty and times of despair,
From powerful medications, debilitating treatments and
    temporary interventions.

Open the hearts of men and women
To share their health
By giving blood,
Registering as marrow donors,
And dedicating themselves to organ donation.
Open, too, the hearts of families
Facing the death of a loved one,
So that, in the shadow of grief,
They find the strength to give the gift of life.
May they find meaning and comfort
In their time of suffering and loss.

God of healing,
[I] [my father/mother/sister/brother/child/wife/husband/
    partner/dear one/friend]
Wait[s] in the shadow of disease,
In the shadow of pain and suffering,
In the shadow of mortality.
May this wait end soon,
With a healthy organ, a successful transplant
And a speedy recovery.

Upon Entering a Clinical Trial

Fountain of life,
My [disease/condition/cancer/_____ (or insert name
    of disease)] has progressed
Beyond the boundaries of proven treatments,
Beyond the limits of medical knowledge,
Beyond the healing arts of physicians.

I am not prepared to surrender.
I am not ready to move on.
I will not accept a conclusion to my treatment.
Instead, I will face the unknown consequences of
Experimental [drugs][and][techniques] to contribute to
    medical science,
Hoping to improve and prolong my life.
I do this for my own sake
And for the sake of medical knowledge.
I do this for the sake of others
And for the sake of Your holy command to choose life.

Bless medical researchers with skill and insight.
Guide them on the path to healing wisdom.
Reveal Your secrets to them
So that my participation yields new treatments
And, one day, a cure.

Blessed are You, God of hope,
God of health and healing,
God of wisdom and wonder.
You call upon us to choose life
In the face of heartache and illness.

Waiting for My Test Results

This moment is familiar.
And this moment is new.
This waiting. This hoping. This praying.
What will the news bring?
What decisions will I face?
How will I cope in the days ahead?

God of old,
Grant me the wisdom to be gentle with myself
In these hours of uncertainty.
Show me the grace and insight to use this time as a moment
    of rest,
Perhaps to find inside myself
A well of gratitude
For the support and comfort of family and friends,
For the wisdom and skill of my doctors,
For the gentle and strong hands of my caregivers.
Surround me with Your warmth.
Cradle me in Your care.

Source of life,
Bless me with courage,
Bless my family with hope,
And lead me on a path to wholeness of body,
Wholeness of mind,
And wholeness of spirit.

Waiting for a Spouse's/Partner's Test Results

God of old,
We wait.
Sometimes in laughter,
Sometimes in tears,
Sometimes in silence.
What will the news bring?
What decisions must be faced?
How will we cope in the days ahead?

Bless my [husband/wife/spouse/partner]
With health and hope.
Grant us the wisdom to be gentle with each other
In these hours of uncertainty.
Show us the grace and insight to use this time as a moment
    of rest,
Perhaps to find a well of gratitude
For the support and comfort of family and friends,
For the wisdom and skill of my doctors,
For the gentle and strong hands of my caregivers.

Source of life,
Surround us with Your warmth.
Cradle _____ [insert name] in Your care.
Lead him/her on a path to wholeness of body,
Wholeness of mind,
And wholeness of spirit.
Bless us with courage
And our family with peace.

Waiting for a Loved One's Test Results

God of old,
Watch over _____ [insert name],
My [father/mother/brother/sister/friend/other relationship],
As he/she waits for test results.
What will the news bring?
What decisions must he/she face?

Source of life,
Bless his/her/our family
With health and hope.
Grant him/her/us solace and rest
In these hours of uncertainty.
Let me be a source of comfort and support
In the hours and days ahead.

God of health and healing,
Surround him/her/us with Your warmth,
And cradle him/her in Your care.
Lead him/her on a path to wholeness of body,
Wholeness of mind,
And wholeness of spirit.
Bless us with courage
And his/her/our family with peace.

ALZHEIMER'S, PARKINSON'S AND DEMENTIA

Diagnosis with Alzheimer's Disease or Dementia

In stages,
I am told,
In stages I will lose my words,
My memories,
My ability to care for myself,
My connection with my family,
My connection with myself.

God of compassion,
Stand with me in the days ahead.
I am [frightened/angry/sad/confused/defiant/(insert a
      description of your emotions)].
Grant me time to remain
Mentally, physically, spiritually and emotionally present
For my family,
For my friends,
And for myself.

Grant healing power to my treatments
To keep this disease at bay.
Give my physicians knowledge and insight
And my caregivers skill and perseverance.
Grant scientists and researchers tools and understanding
To develop new treatments,
Speedily, in our day.

Ancient One,
I need Your care,
Your consolation,
And Your loving hand.

God of old,   קֵל כָּל הַזְּמַנִּים,
You are my Rock and   אַתָּה צוּרִי וְגוֹאֲלִי.
   Redeemer.

El kol haz'manim,
atah tzuri v'go'ali.

Diagnosis with Parkinson's Disease

In stages,
I am told,
In stages I will lose control of my body
And then my mind,
Losing my ability to care for myself
And to hold on to my memories.

God of compassion,
Stand with me in the days ahead.
I am [frightened/angry/sad/confused/defiant/(insert a
    description of your emotions)].
Grant me time to remain
Mentally, physically, spiritually and emotionally present
For my family,
For my friends,
And for myself.

Grant healing power to my treatments
To keep this disease at bay.
Give my physicians knowledge and insight
And my caregivers skill and perseverance.
Grant scientists and researchers tools and understanding
To develop new treatments,
Speedily, in our day.

Ancient One,
I need Your care,
Your consolation,
And Your loving hand.

God of old,   קֵל כָּל הַזְּמַנִּים,
You are my Rock and   אַתָּה צוּרִי וְגוֹאֲלִי.
    Redeemer.

El kol haz'manim,
atah tzuri v'go'ali.

To My Spouse/Partner on My Diagnosis with Alzheimer's or Parkinson's Disease

My darling,
Dear _____ [insert name],
The doctors say that I will be leaving,
Perhaps slowly,
In stages,
[First losing control of my body and then]
Retreating into my mind,
Visiting with you less and less.
It is not my choice to say good-bye.
It is our path.

God of compassion,
Watch over my [husband/wife/spouse/partner]
In the months and years ahead.
Give him/her the strength to live,
To love and to mourn
As we lose each other to this disease.
Grant him/her courage and peace of mind
As we face difficult decisions and difficult moments together
And, in time, he/she faces them without me.

My love,
It is not my choice to leave.
It is not my choice to depart.
It is not my choice to disappear.
Forgive me when my disease
Speaks words of anger or pain.
Remember my devotion to you.
Remember our love and our lives for both of us,
Our joys, our hopes, our dreams.

God of compassion,
Bless my [wife/husband/spouse/partner]
In her/his hours of loss and grief.
And grant her/him a life of wonder and awe
In the years ahead.

This Watching, This Waiting

This watching,
God of old,
This watching my [husband/wife/spouse/partner]
Slowly lose himself/herself to disease
Is a grief beyond my imagination.
Talents and personality,
Plans and dreams,
Moments of conversation,
Moments of pleasure,
Departing stage by stage.

Who is this person inhabiting his/her body?
Where are your memories of our life together?

This waiting,
God of old,
This waiting for the next loss to come
Is a grief beyond my imagination.
Grant me strength and wisdom,
Fortitude and courage,
As the days pass,
As the waiting continues,
As I pray for his/her consolation and peace.

ADDICTION AND MENTAL ILLNESS

My Depression

I have fallen into blackness,
A hole,
A cave without light.
How deep is this pain?
This loneliness?
This suffering and isolation?

God of old,
I call out to You
From the depths of confusion and fear.
What balm will ease my suffering?
What consolation will guide me?
I am afraid and ashamed.
I am sad and lost.

God of healing,
Be the light that guides me
Back to myself,
Back to my joy,
Back to my holiness and wonder.
Help me to stop committing acts of violence against myself
With [self-abuse/anger/shame/food/a blade/alcohol/drugs/sex].
I know Your healing power,
Your salvation and grace.
Lead me on a journey
Back to wholeness and to self-respect.
Help me to live a life of happiness and love.

For an Alcoholic or Addict

God of old,
I call out to You
From the depths of despair.
My [father/mother/sister/brother/son/daughter/friend/
    husband/wife/partner]
Suffers from the disease of [alcoholism/addiction/alcoholism
    and addiction]
[Compounded by mental illness]
Causing harm to himself/herself
And those around him/her.
I am afraid and ashamed.
I am sad and lost.
The disease is powerful.
The possibilities are frightening.

God of health and well-being,
Teach me to care for myself
In the midst of crisis and chaos.
Teach me to bring love and kindness,
Serenity and perspective into my day,
Especially when I feel hopeless or lost.
Teach me to trust Your will.

God of healing,
Bring my [father/mother/sister/brother/son/daughter/friend/
    husband/wife/partner]
In mercy to recovery.
Show him/her Your awesome works
And Your marvelous ways.
Grant him/her healing of body,
Healing of spirit.
Grant relief to all who suffer from alcoholism or addiction,
So that they may become
Living reflections of Your Divine gifts
And Your healing power.

Blessed are You, God of
health and healing.

בָּרוּךְ אַתָּה, אֵל הַבְּרִיאוּת וְהָרְפוּי.

Baruch atah, El hab'ri'ut v'haripuy.

Mental Illness

God of old,
I call out to You
From the depths of confusion and pain.
My [father/mother/sister/brother/son/daughter/friend/
    husband/wife/partner]
Suffers from _____ [insert name of illness]
[Compounded by alcoholism/addiction/alcoholism and
    addiction],
A severe mental illness,
A disease of stunning depth and power.
I am afraid and ashamed.
I am sad and lost.
The possibilities are frightening:
Homelessness, poverty, an institution, jail.
[Sometimes he/she does not take his/her medication.]
[Sometimes he/she threatens me and my family.]
[Sometimes he/she disappears without a trace.]
[Sometimes it looks as though we have lost him/her
    completely to this illness.]

God of healing,
Bless my [father/mother/sister/brother/son/daughter/friend/
    husband/wife/partner] _____ [insert name]
With comfort and relief,
Solace and peace.
Grant him/her healing of mind,
Healing of body,
And healing of spirit.
Teach me to care for myself [and my family]
In the midst of crisis and chaos.
Teach me to bring love and kindness into my day,
Especially when I feel hopeless or lost.
Teach me to trust Your will.

Blessed are You, God of   בָּרוּךְ אַתָּה, קֵל הַבְּרִיאוּת וְהָרִפּוּי.
    health and healing.

Baruch atah, El hab'ri'ut v'haripuy.

My Child's Self-Inflicted Wounds

How deep is her/his pain,
God of old,
That my daughter/son
Commits acts of violence against herself/himself
With [food/a blade/alcohol/drugs/sex]?
I call out to You
From the depths of confusion and fear.
What balm will ease her/his suffering?
What consolation will guide her/his journey
Back to wholeness, to self-respect, to love?

God of healing,
Bless my child
_____ [insert name]
With comfort and well-being,
Solace and relief.
Grant her/him healing of mind,
Healing of body,
And healing of spirit.
Teach me to see her/him through Your eyes,
Eyes of love.
And teach her/him to see the world through Your eyes,
As a place of joy and adventure.

Well of hope,
Grant _____ [insert name]
The ability to be gentle and forgiving to herself/himself.
Lead her/him to new ways of expression,
On a path to happiness and peace.

HOSPICE CARE
AND LETTING GO

Upon Entering Hospice Care

God of All Being,
The well of cures has run dry.
My physicians have been focused,
My caregivers diligent,
My family tireless
In their efforts to help me battle this disease.
The horizon of my life nears.
There is a single destination.

Ancient One,
God of our mothers,
God of our fathers,
I surrender my days to You,
As I must,
With the hopes of a graceful death,
A dignified death,
A loving death.
I make this choice for my own sake,
For the sake of my family and friends,
And for the sake of honoring the life You have given me.

Bless those around me with courage and strength,
Just as I ask You, Holy One,
To grant me the wisdom and ability
To show them my steadfast love,
An inheritance for the generations.

Whatever remains,
The journey hasn't ended.
Ease my pain.
Reduce my suffering.
And bless me, God of my heart,
With days of joy,
With fullness of spirit,
With moments of awe and wonder.

Upon a Loved One's Entering Hospice Care

God of All Being,
The well of cures has run dry.
The physicians have been focused,
The caregivers diligent,
The family tireless
In their efforts to help
My [father/mother/sister/brother/son/daughter/friend/
    husband/wife/partner]
Battle this disease.
The horizon of his/her life nears.
There is a single destination.

Ancient One,
God of our mothers,
God of our fathers,
Look with kindness and favor on
_____ [insert name]
As he/she surrenders his/her days to You.

Bless us with courage and strength,
Just as I ask You, Holy One,
To grant me the wisdom and ability
To show him/her my steadfast love,
An inheritance for the generations.

Whatever remains,
The journey hasn't ended.
Ease his/her pain.
Reduce his/her suffering.
Bless him/her
With days of joy,
With fullness of spirit,
With moments of awe and wonder.

And if it be Your will,
God of old,
Bless him/her with a dignified death,
A loving death,
An easy death.

For My Children as I Enter Hospice Care

My God,
In the days ahead,
The weeks and the months,
I will face challenges as I surrender to _____ [insert
    name of the disease].
My heart and my hopes,
My love and my questions,
Also turn toward my children.
How will they cope?
How will they continue?
How will their experience of my passing
Shape their lives?

This I pray:
In the time that remains,
Let me be a source of love,
A light of comfort,
A lamp of hope,
A well of blessings.
Grant me the ability to care for my children,
Even as they yearn to provide support and understanding
    for me.

[Optional insert: Repeat the following paragraph for each
    child]
Bless my child _____ [insert name],
Who _____ [insert thoughts about what he/she is
    feeling now]
With _____ [insert specific concerns and prayers for
    that child].

God of health and healing,
Watch over my children
In their hour of need.
Watch over them when I have departed.
Let our love for each other
Shine brightly through the days ahead,
So that it lasts beyond the length of my days,
As a testimony to Your Holy Name.

On Removing a Child's Life Support

Before the Removal

Soul of the universe,
When I/we dreamed of becoming [a father/a mother/parents],
I/We never expected to face the death of [my/our] [son/
    daughter],
Who is still [only a baby/child/youth/teen] [in (his/her) prime],
To remove life support,
And, in days to come, to bury him/her.
You have challenged me/us to make painful choices,
Unimaginable choices,
And yet, God of Ages, benevolent and holy choices.

I/We do this in the name of healing.
    And I/we do this in the name of kindness.
I/We do this in the name of mercy.
    And I/we do this in the name of grace.
I/We do this in the name of love.
    And I/we do this in the name of compassion.
I/We do this from the depths our despair,
    Praying to find a path back to wholeness and life renewed.

After Passing

Author of life,
Source and Creator,
Grant a perfect rest under Your tabernacle of peace to
_____ [insert name],
My/Our child,
Whose life has ended too soon.
May the memory of [my/our] [son/daughter] be sanctified
    with joy and love.
May his/her soul be bound up in the bond of life,
A source of blessing in our midst.

MEDICAL SCIENCE AND MEDICAL PROFESSIONALS

For Physicians

God of old,
We are flesh and blood,
Imbued with Your Divine spark,
Strong but vulnerable.
You have blessed us with men and women
Who dedicate their lives to health and healing,
Preventing disease, reducing pain,
Prolonging lives, providing hope.

God of life,
Watch over our physicians
And all who work in the healing professions
As they serve us during times of health and
In the times of our deepest needs.
Bless their hands with kindness,
Their eyes with courage,
Their hearts with sincerity,
And their souls with love,
So that they become
A fountain of healing.
Bless them with fortitude and strength.

Rock of Ages,
Bring an end to pain and suffering,
So that all may know
Your compassion and Your grace.

Bless doctors throughout the world
With Your warmth and shelter,
Even as we bless them
With our eternal gratitude and love.

For Nurses

To those who dedicate their lives to compassion,
To those who dedicate their lives to care,
To those who hold our hearts and spirits dear:
    Your work is a blessing,
    Your days are a gift,
    Your hours are a labor of holiness,
    Your moments are a well of comfort.

God of life,
Watch over our nurses
And all who work in the healing professions
As they serve us in the times of our deepest needs.
Bless their hands with kindness,
Their eyes with courage,
Their hearts with sincerity,
And their souls with love,
So that they become
A fountain of healing.
Bless them with fortitude and strength.
Grant them satisfaction and success at work,
Joy and rest,
Security and peace in their lives.

Rock of Ages,
Bring an end to pain and suffering,
So that all may know
Your compassion and Your grace.

Bless all who serve in the nursing professions
With Your warmth and shelter,
Even as we bless them
With our eternal gratitude and love.

For My Nurses, Therapists and Aides

God of healing,
Watch over me during this time of [convalescence/treatment/
    recuperation/therapy/decline]
As I move toward [recovery/rebuilding my life/accepting
    new limitations/the end of my life].

Thank You,
God of compassion,
For the gift of my nurses, therapists and aides,
Those who have dedicated themselves to my care.
Their work is a blessing,
Their days and hours are a gift of holiness,
A well of hope and comfort in my life.
Bless them with fortitude and strength,
Just as You have blessed me with
Their hands of kindness,
Their eyes of courage,
Their hearts of sincerity and love.

Grant them satisfaction and success,
Joy and rest,
Security and peace,
So that they remain
A fountain of healing.

Rock of Ages,
Bring an end to pain and suffering,
So that all may know
Your compassion and Your grace.

Bless all of those who serve in the caring professions
With Your warmth and shelter,
Even as we bless them
With our eternal gratitude and love.

For Medical Science

God of wisdom,
We give thanks for the fruit of medical science,
The gifts of health and healing
That have saved millions of people:
From immunization to chemotherapy,
From diagnostics to surgery.
You gave us the tools of science and research,
Intelligence and curiosity,
Challenging us to be Your partner
In bringing new medications and remedies,
Technologies and procedures,
Into the world.
The needs are great.
Diseases and conditions still plague
The lives of our families,
Our brothers and sisters,
Nations and communities,
Young and old.

God of love,
Bless medical scientists and researchers with
Insight and skill,
Dedication and fortitude,
So that their work yields knowledge and understanding
Leading to new treatments and cures,
Speedily, in our day.
Grant medical science the wisdom to use these gifts wisely
In service to the highest ideals of humankind.

Rock of Ages,
Bring an end to pain and suffering,
So that all may know
Your compassion and Your grace.

Blessed are You, God of   בָּרוּךְ אַתָּה, קֵל הַבְּרִיאוּת וְהָרְפוּי.
    health and healing.

Baruch atah, El hab'ri'ut v'haripuy.

For Organ Donation

God of health and healing,
We give thanks for the medical science
That allows us to remove organs from one person
And implant them into another,
Renewing life for the critically ill.

Bless all those who dedicate their lives to this sacred task.
Grant strength and fortitude to the scientists and researchers,
Surgeons, nurses and clinicians,
Administrators and other professionals
Whose efforts give life.
May the work of their hands never falter.

Shine Your light on those who,
Still living, give so freely of themselves.
Grant them health, prosperity and long life.

Remember those who have given of themselves in death,
Providing vital organs to those on the edge of life.
May this final act of charity and love
Be a testimony to their lives.
Grant their families comfort, consolation and peace.

Blessed are You, God
of miracles,
Who heals, blesses and
sustains life.

בָּרוּךְ אַתָּה, קֵל הַנִּסִּים,
הַמְּרַפֵּא, מְבָרֵךְ וּמְכַלְכֵּל חַיִּים בְּחֶסֶד.

Baruch atah, El hanisim,
ham'rapei, m'vareich u'm'chalkeil chayim b'chesed.

For Organ and Tissue Donation

God of health and healing,
We give thanks for the medical science
That allows us to remove organs and tissue from one person
And implant them into another,
Renewing life for the critically ill.

Bless all those who dedicate their lives to this sacred task.
Grant strength and fortitude to the scientists and researchers,
Surgeons, nurses and clinicians,
Administrators and other professionals
Whose efforts give life.
May the work of their hands never falter.

Shine Your light on those who,
Still living, give so freely of themselves.
Grant them health, prosperity and long life.

Remember those who have given of themselves in death.
May this final act of charity and love
Be a testimony to their lives.
Grant their families comfort, consolation and peace.

Blessed are You, God   בָּרוּךְ אַתָּה, קֵל הַנִּסִּים,
 of miracles,   הַמְרַפֵּא, מְבָרֵךְ וּמְכַלְכֵּל חַיִּים בְּחֶסֶד.
Who heals, blesses and
 sustains life.

Baruch atah, El hanisim,
ham'rapei, m'vareich u'm'chalkeil chayim b'chesed.

HEALING THE SOUL

SORROWS

For Healing the Spirit

Daughter of man,
Son of woman,
Children of love and Divine union:
Why do you stay buried in your losses,
    Crushed by your burdens,
    Drowned by your fears?
Why do you look down to the dust
    When the morning sky
    Bursts with daybreak?
    When the night
    Shimmers with starlight?
Why do you shuffle your feet
    When the earth calls out
    To feel your dance?
Daughter of majestic gifts,
Son of glorious secrets:
    Cast off your sorrows.
    Banish your pain.
    Exile your grief.
There is joy in every breath,
Mystery in every sky.

Come you children of God,
You witnesses of life and loss:
Walk with dignity toward holiness
    And with grace toward healing.
Walk with confidence into each moment
    And with passion into each new day.
Then your lives will become a blessing,
A Divine teacher,
An instrument of heaven,
A messenger of hope.

Blessed are You,
  Creator of life,
You heal the broken
  spirit with love.

בָּרוּךְ אַתָּה, בּוֹרֵא הַחַיִּים,
אַתָּה מְרַפֵּא שְׁבוּרֵי לֵב בְּאַהֲבָה.

Baruch atah, borei hachayim,
atah m'rapei sh'vurei leiv b'ahavah.

R'fu'at Hanefesh

God of the spirit,
God of the soul, the breath and the wind,
Look with kindness and favor on _____ [insert name],
My [father/mother/sister/brother/son/daughter/friend/
    husband/wife/partner],
Whose heart aches,
Crushed and fallow,
Whose heart yearns,
Empty and broken.
God of the *nefesh*, *ruach* and *neshama*,
Guide his/her soul
Back to wonder and mystery,
Sacred moments and glorious days,
So that he/she knows the power of Your love
And the wisdom of Your word.
May his/her soul shine,
A light and blessing
For our people Israel.

For Sharing Divine Gifts

Daughter of man,
Son of woman,
People of Divine light:
What do you do with your gifts?
    How do you use your radiance
    And your might?
    Your intellect and your passion?
Do you leave them buried within,
    Untouched and unused?
    Do you pursue justice and healing,
    Charity and consolation?
Men of honor and purpose,
Women of integrity and strength:
    Cast off your idle ways.
    Banish your selfish pursuits.
    Exile your vain hopes.
There is joy in every kindness,
Blessing and salvation in every gift of the heart.

Come you children of God,
You witnesses of wonder and awe,
There are miracles inside you,
    Holy gifts of communion and grace
    That yearn to burst forth in celebration of God's Holy
      Name.
    Answer the call to Divine service.
Then your lives will become a blessing,
A well a love,
A source of splendor,
Abundant in joy and courage.

Blessed are You, Source   בָּרוּךְ אַתָּה, מְקוֹר הַמַּתָּנוֹת הַפְּלִאִיּוֹת,
   of miraculous gifts,   הַשָּׂמֵחַ בְּמַעֲשֵׂי לֵב.
You rejoice in deeds
   of the heart.

Baruch atah, m'kor hamatanot hapil'iyot,
hasamei'ach b'ma'asei leiv.

Carry Me

God, carry me today,
With Your love,
Your grace,
Your wisdom and strength.
God, carry me today,
With Your power,
Your justice,
Your holiness and law.
God, carry me today,
Through stormy winds and rough seas,
The obvious and unforeseen
Challenges and losses,
The uneven flow of my emotions,
My fears and my shames.

Today, God on high,
I will not succeed alone.
I will not survive alone.
I need Your majesty and might,
Your dignity and righteousness,
To carry me through the day ahead.
With You as my Rock and Shield,
I will face this day with an answer
To loneliness and dread,
Misgivings and mistakes,
To stand with courage and freedom
Against misfortune and deceit.

God, carry me today.
Give me healing hands,
A quiet mind,
Gentle speech,
And a forgiving heart.
Let me feel You in my chest.
Let me feel You in my limbs.
Let me feel You by my side.

Blessed are You, God of All,
You are the answer to
those in need.

בָּרוּךְ אַתָּה, קֵל הַכֹּל,
אַתָּה הַמַּעֲנֶה לְכָל נִזְקָק.

Baruch atah, El hakol,
atah hama'aneh l'chol nizkak.

Season of Sorrow

This is my season of sorrow.
A time when struggles begin,
When challenges arrive,
When endings occur.
Moments of pain.
Moments of sadness.
Moments of confusion.
Times of loss. Times of grief.
Moments that stripped me of wisdom
And left me crushed and breathless,
Cold and in deepening shadow.

Holy One,
Help me recall my seasons of joy
To recall with hope and praise
Your gifts and blessings.
Moments of laughter.
Moments of kindness.
Moments of peace.
Times of health. Times of clarity.
Moments that lifted my spirit
And comforted my heart.

In truth,
These joys and sorrows
Are gifts of holiness,
Gifts of mystery,
Gifts beyond my wisdom,
My knowledge,
My understanding.

Rock of Old,
You are my comfort
   and my strength,
My light and my truth.

צוּר עוֹלָמִים,
אַתָּה נֶחָמָתִי וְכֹחִי,
אוֹרִי וַאֲמִתִּי.

Tzur olamim,
atah nechamati v'chochi,
ori va'amiti.

Regarding Old Wounds

Daughter of man,
Son of woman,
Children of compassion and sacred secrets:
Your wounds are deep,
  Your losses crushing,
  Knife on flesh,
  Hammer on bone,
  Burning your heart and searing your eyes.
Why do you invite them back
  To chastise your days
  And torture your nights?
Why do you love these old wounds,
  Holding them so dear?
Son of celebration,
Daughter of ecstasy:
  Cast off your doubts,
  Banish your fears,
  Exile the pain of time beyond your reach.
There is beauty in your past,
Wonder in your future,
And holiness in each new moment of life.

Come you children of God,
You witnesses of suffering and grace,
  Lift your heads from your hands,
  Raise your voices in song,
  Lift your lives in service,
  And rekindle the light of compassion and love.
Then your lives will become a blessing,
A well of hope,
A river of consolation,
A fountain of peace.

Blessed are You, God
  of forgiveness,
You renew our lives
  with purpose.

בָּרוּךְ אַתָּה, קֵל הַסְּלִיחוֹת,
הַמְחַדֵּשׁ אֶת חַיֵּינוּ בִּתְחוּשָׁה שֶׁל יִעוּד.

Baruch atah, El has'lichot,
ham'chadeish et chayeinu bit'chushah shel yi'ud.

BEREAVEMENTS

For the Bereaved

Rock of Jacob,
Comfort of Rachel,
Broken and torn,
Shattered and crushed,
Bereaved and bereft,
We declare Your Holy Name.

We praise Your gifts and Your works.
You are Author and Artist,
Architect and Builder,
Source and Redeemer.

We the mourners of Zion and Israel
Comfort each other.
We console the lonely and embrace the lost.
We cry each other's tears.
Together we recall Your wonder and Your majesty.

Holy One,	קָדוֹשׁ אַתָּה,
Ineffable Redeemer,	מוֹשִׁיעַ וְאֵין בִּלְתּוֹ,
Guiding hand,	בְּיָד מוֹבִילָה,
Gentle hand,	בְּיָד עֲדִינָה,
Loving hand,	בְּיָד אוֹהֶבֶת,
Light of Israel,	אוֹר יִשְׂרָאֵל,
Guardian of Israel.	שׁוֹמֵר יִשְׂרָאֵל.

Kadosh atah,
moshi'a v'ein bilto,
b'yad movilah,
b'yad adinah,
b'yad ohevet,
Or Yisrael,
Shomeir Yisrael.

For Bereaved Children

Father of Jacob,
Mother of Rachel,
Source of awe and wonder,
Cradle and Shelter,
Our children are lost in tears,
Crushed in sorrow,
Erased in loneliness,
Bent and broken,
Their hopes, dust . . .
Their joys, cinders . . .
Their dreams, shadows.

You who comfort Zion and Israel,
Comfort our children in this moment of grievous loss,
And show them the path from darkness to light.
Renew their hope,
Rekindle their joy,
Spark their dreams,
So that they, too, will know Your healing power,
Your salvation and grace,
Your loving-kindness.
Hold them,
Lift them,
Carry them,
Until, refreshed by Your spirit,
They walk upright once again,
Toward holiness and love,
With charity and thanksgiving,
Humility and strength,
In awe and righteousness,
To sing Your praise.

After Shiva

The days have passed,
And a quiet has settled on my home.
My grief still holds me.
My sorrow is present.
Yet You, God of seasons,
Ask me to look gently
Toward the future.
You, God of creation,
Ask me to imagine a time
When the pain begins to fade,
A time when my hopes are renewed.
You, God of generations,
Ask me to honor life,
To cherish memory,
To love those who remain.

Source and Shelter,
Loving Guide of the bereaved,
Lead me on the path toward
Wholeness and healing,
Peace and comfort,
So that I become a well
Of compassion and strength.

God of old,
Your ways are secret,
Sacred and holy.
You are my Rock.
You are my Lamp.

Blessed are You,
God of All,
Who redeems the bereaved
    with love.

בָּרוּךְ אַתָּה, קֵל הַכֹּל,
הַגּוֹאֵל אֲבֵלִים בְּאַהֲבָה.

Baruch atah, El hakol,
hago'eil aveilim b'ahavah.

This Wound

God of my heart,
This wound is too deep for me to heal
Without You,
Your power and Your grace.
Remove the walls of grief that separate me from
Your love and Your blessings.
You call us to life,
To hope,
To service,
To seek and to do,
To heal and to complete Your creation.

God of gentle moments,
I surrender my life to
Your awesome works,
Your secret ways.
Reunite me with myself,
With my fellows,
And with the world
To do Your will in humble service.

Blessed are You, Your   בָּרוּךְ אַתָּה, אַהֲבָתְךָ נִצְחִית.
    love is eternal.

Baruch atah, ahavat'cha nitzchit.

Shall I Cry?

Shall I cry at the last withered leaf of fall?
Or the lonely swallow?
Or my grieving heart?

Shall I mourn the past?
Protest the future?
Bury myself in these losses?
The leaving. The death.

Oh you sea of clouds.
Oh you curtain of rain.
Oh you silent yearning.
You arrive as messenger and guide,
Sent from the Source of healing,
The Source of radiance and wonder.

This soul cannot learn to love
In heaven, where only
The vast blue glory
Of light
Resides.

SURRENDER

Life as a Garden

God of majestic moments,
Source of splendor,
Creator of radiance,
Divine light of renewal and joy,
  My knowledge has its limits,
  My insights are fleeting,
  My wisdom emanates from an ancient font of holiness
    and wonder.
  What I witness and what I comprehend are blessings and
    gifts.

Heavenly hand of possibilities and potential,
Artist of all creation,
Grant me the dignity to live my life as a garden,
Planting moments of kindness and grace,
Gently removing the thorns and bramble,
Nourishing each new blessing with the light of love and peace.

You who bring awareness and understanding,
  Guide me with purpose,
  Teach me with patience,
  Show me the gentle path,
So that I live a life of commitment and devotion,
In celebration of Your creation.

Blessed are You, *Adonai*
  our God,
God of life, Author of
  beauty and grandeur.

בָּרוּךְ אַתָּה ה' אֱלֹקֵינוּ,
קֵל הַחַיִּים, בּוֹרֵא הַיֹּפִי וְהַתִּפְאָרֶת.

*Baruch atah Adonai Eloheinu,
El hachayim, borei hayofi v'hatif'eret.*

169

Life as a Ceremony

God of the past,
Source of the present,
Creator of the future,
Divine light of compassion and hope,
    My time is fleeting.
    My days are numbered.
    The course of my life unknown.
    Where I am and where I'll be a mystery.

Heavenly hand of justice and mercy,
Keeper of secret truths,
You who give purpose and meaning to all things,
Grant me the grace and vision to live my life as a ceremony,
As a river of sacred moments that command my care,
That I honor with love and respect.
Give me the wisdom to see the spark,
The splendor and the spirit around me,
And to choose the path of enthusiasm, energy, gentleness
    and peace.

You who know all things,
    Guide me with Your wisdom,
    Teach me Your laws,
    Show me Your ways,
So that I live a life of joy and holiness,
Treating everyone and everything with dignity and honor,
In service to Your creation.

Blessed are You, God of All,   בָּרוּךְ אַתָּה, קֵל הַכֹּל,
Source of life and love,   מְקוֹר חַיִּים וְאַהֲבָה, שֶׁפַע וְשָׁלוֹם.
    abundance and peace.

Baruch atah, El hakol,
m'kor chayim v'ahavah, shefa v'shalom.

Life as a Banquet

God of sacred time,
Source of sacred space,
Creator of holiness,
Divine light of wonder and awe,
My vision is clouded,
My sight limited,
The horizon of this world binds my perceptions.
What I see and what I know are tied to my awareness.

Heavenly hand of wisdom,
Guardian of realms above and realms below,
You who give understanding and insight,
Grant me the grace to live my life as a banquet,
A river of abundance and blessing
That yields food and clothing and shelter,
That I accept with humility and thanksgiving.
Give me the strength and compassion
To share these gifts with those in need,
To become an instrument of Divine bounty.

You who provide gifts beyond measure,
Guide me with Your love,
Teach me with Your holiness,
Show me the path to charity and service,
So that I live a life of dignity and honor,
With reverence for Your creation.

Blessed are You, God of   בָּרוּךְ אַתָּה, קֵל הַזְּמַן וְהַמָּקוֹם,
time and space,   נוֹתֵן שֶׁפַע כְּדֵי שֶׁנַּשְׁפִּיעַ זֶה לָזֶה.
Providing bounty to
be shared.

Baruch atah, El haz'man v'hamakom,
notein shefa k'dei shenashpi'a zeh lazeh.

Life as a Symphony

God of ancient secrets,
Source of life,
Creator of beauty,
Divine light of sacred truth,
    My strength has its limits,
    My power its purpose,
    The energy of life flowing from a secret well beyond my
        reach
    And beyond my imagination.
    What I find and what finds me are a mystery and a
        miracle.

Heavenly hand of radiance and hope,
Author of All Being,
Grant me the wisdom and understanding to live my life as a
    symphony,
A river of majestic music that blesses and sustains
With holiness and love,
That I repay with kindness and charity.
Give me the passion and the patience to hear the rhythms of
    Your glorious creation.

You who bring beauty and song,
    Guide me with Your power,
    Teach me with Your kindness,
    Show me the reverence for Your secret truths,
So that I live a life of joy and celebration,
With gratitude for Your creation.

Blessed are You, God of   בָּרוּךְ אַתָּה, קֵל הַיְשׁוּעָה וְהָרוֹמְמוּת,
    salvation and splendor,   תְּשִׁירְךָ וּתְהַלֶּלְךָ הַבְּרִיאָה.
Creation sings Your praise.

Baruch atah, El hay'shu'ah v'harom'mut,
t'shircha u't'halelcha hab'ri'ah.

In Plain Sight

Ancient One,
God of old,
Teacher, Guide and Shelter,
Your gifts are hidden in plain sight.
Why do I struggle to see
Love and light,
Hope and tomorrow,
The moment that just was,
And the moment that will be?
My warm breath
And my grieving heart.
The gifts of this life.

Source of All Being,
Grant me the vision to see the gifts around me,
The wisdom to share Your bounty and grace,
And the humility to praise Your Holy Name.

The Open Space

Wholeness is the open space,
   The place between,
      Where the rhythm of being
         Enters, flows through,
            In my vision and my courage.

Forgiveness is the open space,
   Where yesterday meets tomorrow,
      Where the tide waits to shift
         Where holiness blesses the mundane,
            In my breath and my celebration.

Wisdom is the open space,
   Where the echo hears the wind,
      Where the silence becomes God's voice
         Where all that I am meets all that I can be,
            In my marrow and in my surrender.

This Moment

How did I arrive in this place?
This joy and wonder.
This grief and loss.
This hour. This moment. This life.
Choices. Events. God.
My decisions. The decisions of others.
The hand of our Creator.

Holy One,
Help me to see that I am exactly
Where I need to be
To learn and to serve,
To be and to become,
To live as an instrument of healing and love,
Charity and forgiveness,
Kindness and grace.

How did I arrive in this moment?
How did I get this blessing,
This gift,
To be exactly where I can learn and serve
In God's Holy Name?

Whispered Prayer

Your whispered prayer,
Your secret hope,
Your quiet yearning
Have holiness and power.
They resound in the heavens
And echo on high.
They are drum and cymbal,
Trumpet and horn,
Proclaiming your faith,
Music of generations,
Proclaiming your hope,
Hymns of the heart,
Proclaiming your dedication
To the God of All Being,
Source and Shelter,
Rock and Redeemer,
Light and Truth.

Your whispered prayer
Is the song of the ages.
Your secret hope
Is the light of tomorrow.
Your quiet yearning
Is the voice of eternity.

Blessed are You, *Adonai*,   בָּרוּךְ אַתָּה ה', שׁוֹמֵעַ תְּפִלָּה.
 who hears prayer.

Baruch atah Adonai, shomei'a t'filah.

ACKNOWLEDGMENTS

God of creativity,
Heavenly hand of beauty and wonder,
Bless those who have supported me,
Helped and encouraged me,
Sharing their wisdom and talents
As I pursue the call to write
In service to Your Holy Name.
You have sent men and women,
Teachers and counselors,
Friends and guides,
To travel with me on this journey of prayer and blessing.
May their enthusiasm return to them, tenfold, as gifts.
May their wisdom continue to echo into the world
And into the lives of those around them,
Yielding holiness and love in the light of their presence.
Bless them, sustain them and grant them
Health and happiness,
Joy and peace.

Thanks to those of you who've supported me by reading my prayers and poetry regularly online. Seeing my readership grow gives me confidence and joy as I explore deeper and more challenging topics and as I experiment with a wide variety of voices for prayer. Thanks also to those who supported my Kickstarter campaign.

Thanks to all of you who've supported and encouraged my development as a liturgist. Some provided a simple but important moment of encouragement, while others created opportunities for me to write. Some offered comment when I was challenged by a particular prayer. Still others suggested topics for me to address. I am blessed with your light and your wisdom, as well as a list far too long to include. Among them, whether they know it or not, several had a direct impact on my writing and this book: Rabbi Ruth Abusch-Magder, Asher Arbit, Sophie Black, Rabbi Erin Boxt, Rabbi Bob Carroll, Rabbi Stephanie Clark Covitz, Dr. Robyne Diller, Brenda Epstein, Cantor Liat Pelman-Forst, Cantor Erin Miles Frankel, Tracy Friend, Michael P. Greenwald, Deborah Greniman, Larry Horberg, *z"l*, Rabbi Dana Evan Kaplan, Larry Kaufman, *z"l*, Rabbi Karyn Kedar, Irwin Keller, Cantor Evan Kent, Rabbi Paul Kipnes, Rabbi Hanna Klebansky, Cantor Jeff Klepper, Rabbi Peter Knobel, Ira Scott Levin, Julia Bordenaro Levin, Rabbi Rebecca Lillian, Rabbi Andrea London, Mara Lund, Michal Malen, Rabbi Hara Person, Rhonda Rosenheck, Roslyn Roucher, Roberta Schweitzer, Blair Solovy, Andrew David Sussman, Joe Tye, Elisheva Urbas and Aaron Wickenden. Let me apologize, in advance, to anyone whom I've inadvertently missed.

I'm touched deeply by six people who read this book and provided heartfelt words of support. Four very special endorsements came from Rev. Dr. Margaret Benefiel, Susan Diamond, Pastor Austin Fleming and Rabbi David Levin-Kruss. Two lovely and touching introductions, written by Rabbi Susan Silverman and Rabbi William H. Lebeau, set the tone for readers. Your words are joyous for me to read. Your continued support is humbling to receive. Thank you all.

A word of thanks to those who had a direct hand in turning my work into this book: simply, you helped me fulfill a dream. In this way, you have blessed me. Thanks to my Hebrew team, who provided the translations, transliterations and *nikud*: Ruth Noy and Chava Katz. Thanks to my crack copyeditor and proofreader, Janice Meyerson. Special thanks to Mayapriya Long, the designer, and Martin Sykes-Haas, the cover photographer. Your work creates an inviting visual space for prayer. Fern Reiss provided invaluable coaching and advice throughout the process. Without her, there would be no book.

My family blesses me at every turn. Thank you to my father Jack, $z"l$, and my Uncle Jerry, $z"l$, for teaching me the value of family and meaningful work. I've received steadfast support for pursuing my dreams from my daughters and my mother. Your love is abundant. To my mom, thanks for encouraging my journey. To my girls, thanks for your help with this project and your enthusiasm. I know that your mom, $z"l$, is proud of you. I am, too.

READER'S GUIDE

SUMMARY

This volume contains a wide variety of prayers for use in our daily lives. These prayers focus on times of joy and times of challenge. They address issues we may face as our lives progress—triumphs and tragedies, ranging from family celebrations to personal illness, from birth to death, from love to loneliness. All these prayers are inspired by Jewish faith and practice, although most of them have universal themes and use generally universal language, with the inclusion of Hebrew terms and Jewish concepts, such as *tikun olam* ("repairing the world"). Other prayers in this volume are "classically" Jewish, tied to the themes of holidays and seasons in Jewish life or reflecting core Jewish ideas, culture or theology. The prayers in this book are divided into three major categories: A Life of Meaning, Healing the Body and Healing the Soul.

QUESTIONS FOR DISCUSSION

About Prayer

1. The use of articulation—song, speech—is the classic form of prayer as practiced in Western cultures. Are there other ways to pray? Can an act of charity be a prayer? Can visiting the sick? Or studying spiritual or religious teaching? Silence? Meditation? Is the intention of bringing healing, beauty or love into the world—without the use of words to mark the moment—enough to be considered a prayer? What is the role of words in making a prayer meaningful?

2. What are the essential elements of a formal prayer? Words? Music? Can it be a more general yearning of the heart? Or perhaps prayer is simply a special kind of awareness, a different attitude that a person brings to the relationship between God and humanity. Does prayer always include a specific communication with God or a specific request of God?

3. The introduction makes a distinction between prayers and blessings, using light as a metaphor, stating that prayer is an act of *summoning light* and that blessing is an act of *bending light*. "Light is a universal metaphor for Divine energy, a symbol for holiness, truth, radiance, eminence, love," the Introduction notes. "To pray is to summon Divine light into our lives. To bless is an attempt to summon that light and then to bend it toward holy purpose, including consolation, healing, joy and peace." Is there a difference between a prayer and a blessing? If so, when is it necessary or appropriate to pray? When is it appropriate or necessary to recite a blessing?

4. Meditation is another tool often used to connect with holiness, divinity, an inner voice, the voice of God. What is the difference between prayer and meditation? Do they play different roles in the religious or the spiritual journey? Do they have different effects on those who pray or meditate? What role do words play in the effective use of various meditation techniques, such as repeating a mantra or hearing imagery in a guided meditation?

5. Does the act of prayer change the person who is praying? If so, in what ways? How does this effect on the person who is praying influence the nature of prayer and the role of prayer in connecting with holiness? In other words, is the intent of prayer to change the hand of God or to change the attitude and perspective of the person who is praying?

6. There are four classic types of prayer: praise, petition, gratitude and forgiveness. These forms of prayer have also been categories using simpler, less theological language, such as: "wow," "gimme," "thanks" and "oops." What is the role of each of these types of prayer? Which of them are more meaningful or less meaningful to you? Why does a particular type of prayer resonate more strongly for you? Is there an essential element of this form of prayer that is more natural for you—more connected with the way you think?

7. Praise—the "wow!" prayer—states the wonder and awe of God's works and God's world. Of course, God already knows this. And certainly, anyone reciting such a prayer does, too. It can be said, then, that neither God nor human beings need these prayers of praise. Yet spiritual and religious individuals yearn to declare the beauty and holiness in the world. Some do it with words, specifically in prayer or with poetry and song. Others create art, photography, dance or music—even mathematics and science—to express beauty and other emotions. There appears to be a fundamental spiritual and religious belief among many that God also wants to hear these praises. What is the role of praising God in prayer? Do we need these prayers? Does God? How does your answer influence your conception of God? How does your answer influence your conception of prayer?

8. Petition—asking for God's direct intercession in a moment or a situation, also called the "gimme" prayer—has been part of private and communal prayer for centuries. Do you believe that prayer can change the course of an individual illness or bring relief to a particular person? Can prayers of petition bring changes to the world at large, perhaps resulting in the end of a war or relieving

the suffering from a major calamity, such as a famine or a natural disaster?

9. In biblical times—and even in modern times—some people connected illness and tragedy with punishment from God. Although this is a less popular concept today, some healing prayers written as recently as the mid-twentieth century included asking God to forgive the sins of the person afflicted with disease or to remember the virtues of that individual. Do you believe that there is a connection between illness and punishment from God? If so, can all tragedy be explained by punishment for sin? How does your answer influence your conception of God? How does your answer influence your conception of prayer?

10. What is the role of gratitude—the "thanks" prayer—in communication with God? What role does acknowledging God's gift play in creating gratitude among those who pray? Is thanking God for the blessings of daily life an essential part of a daily prayer practice? Is the act of thanking God after moments of struggle and challenge more important or less important than prayers of petition?

11. Is there a relationship between prayers of gratitude or praise and prayers of petition? In other words, is there a connection between reciting prayers of thanks or praise and whether God will listen to prayers of petition in the future? How does your answer influence your concept of God? How does your answer influence your concept of prayer?

12. Asking for forgiveness—the "oops" prayer—is a key part of Jewish and other Western religious liturgy. What types of actions should be addressed with the "oops"? Can these prayers play a role in repairing any damage that the action(s) may have done to others or the world? What

about the person who made the mistake or hurt someone? Can these prayers play a role in repairing the spiritual damage done to the person who must ask for forgiveness?

About the Prayers in This Book

13. The title of this volume is *Jewish Prayers of Hope and Healing.* What is the difference between a prayer of hope and a prayer of healing? Can a prayer of hope bring healing? Can a prayer of healing bring hope? What is the connection between hope and healing in prayer?

14. This volume uses words to summon emotions, and it uses verbal imagery in creating communication with God. What is the role of verbal imagery in creating a meaningful prayer? How important is the emotional component of the prayer?

15. Some prayers in this volume sound like liturgical pieces, while others read more like songs, poems or meditations. Is the language key to whether a prayer is meaningful for you? Is the language key to whether you will use a particular prayer? What form do you prefer: liturgical prayer, poem, song or meditation?

16. These prayers are, for the most part, focused on private moments of prayer, rather than on organized, communal prayer in, for example, a church, synagogue or mosque. Is private prayer more powerful or less powerful than communal prayer? Which resonates more strongly for you: private prayer or communal prayer?

17. Which prayers in this volume feel universal and which feel strongly influenced by a Jewish perspective, specifically focused on that one faith? How does the Jewish aspect of some of the prayers influence your relationship to that prayer? Are the words more meaningful or less

meaningful, or is it irrelevant to whether a particular prayer in this book resonates with you?

About Your Life of Prayer

18. What is the role of prayer in your life? Are you more likely to pray when you face challenges or struggles? Are you more likely to pray for yourself or for someone else? What situations make you more likely to pray?
19. Do you participate in regular organized prayer at a religious institution? Why or why not? What do you find most meaningful: personal prayer; informal prayer in small groups; organized formal prayer groups; or organized prayer that is part of a religious institution? What are the positive elements of individual and communal prayer settings? What are the drawbacks?
20. Do you pray together with your family outside organized institutional prayer, such as before a meal or when a family member is sick? Do you pray in private groups with friends? If so, under what circumstances?
21. When do you pray? How often do you pray? Do you have a daily or weekly prayer or meditation practice? Do you pray before meals? After meals? Do you pray before you go to sleep? Do you pray when you wake up?
22. Have you participated in formal prayer in informal settings—for example, a formal synagogue or church service held in a forest or on a beach? How do these settings change your relationship to prayer? Do you have a story of formal prayer in an informal setting? Describe the purpose of the prayer service: what was going on, who was with you, what happened, how you felt and how being outside a formal setting influenced the mood of prayer. Did you feel more connected or less connected to prayer in that setting?

23. Does someone need to believe in God in order to pray? Is it necessary to believe in God for prayer to "work"? What does it mean for prayer to "work"? Do you personally believe in God? Have you believed in God your entire life? How has your concept of God changed over the years? Can you pray for someone who doesn't believe in God?

24. Do you experience prayer as a source of hope for you or others in your life? Do you experience prayer as a source of healing for you or others in your life? Do you believe that the act of prayer can generate health or prolong life?

25. What is the most powerful or memorable moment of prayer that you have experienced? Describe what was going on, who was with you, what happened, how you felt during that moment, and how you felt later in the day, several hours after the moment had passed. Have you shared this experience before? If not, how does it feel to describe what took place? What does it mean to you to share this experience?

26. If you are Jewish, what aspects of these prayers sound and feel Jewish to you? What aspects feel either more universal or not particularly Jewish to you? If you are not Jewish, did some of these prayers sound or feel different from the prayers of your faith tradition? How does the inclusion of Hebrew words and phrases influence your ability to use these prayers? Do you feel more connected to the prayers with explicit Jewish references or to the ones without?

Science and Prayer

27. Scientists have begun to focus more medical research on the effect of prayer on health. According to WebMD, by 2004 more than 1,200 studies had been conducted on the

relationship between prayer and personal health; that is, how an individual's prayer and meditation life influences his or her health. The general conclusion is that those who pray and meditate live healthier and happier lives. Do you agree? Do you have evidence of this in your own life or stories that you are willing to share?

28. A 2006 study of intercessory prayer—prayers said on behalf of someone else—found no scientifically measurable connection between prayers said for someone else and medical outcomes. Published in the *American Heart Journal*, it was the largest study of prayer and healing, including more than 1,800 coronary artery bypass graft surgery patients. It followed a controversial study that claimed to find a connection but was later shown to be flawed in its methods. Do you believe that prayers on behalf of someone else can influence that person's health, happiness, well-being or longevity? Is that belief part of your faith or religion, or does it come from your personal experiences?

29. In keeping with the Jewish belief in the power of prayer—that "petitions" are heard by God and may be answered—this book includes a variety of prayers for healing. What does your faith tradition say about the relationship between petitionary prayer and healing? How has that theology influenced your beliefs and practices? Does it make a difference if one, 10 or 100 people are praying for an individual? Does it make a difference if the prayer is recited by one individual over and over again?

AUTHOR INTERVIEW

Q. The topics of the prayers in this book are universal, from health and healing to family matters and meditations on love and death. Yet you are clear that these are Jewish prayers of hope and healing. The title of the book makes the point. What makes these prayers particularly Jewish?

Prayer binds people of all faiths. With little effort, we can find prayers from all faiths that speak to our hearts. We can also find meditations written by those who describe themselves as spiritual but not religious that speak to our common human experience, our common human desires and our common human path. The themes in my prayers touch the universal moments of prayer: life and death, joy and sorrow, actual events in our lives and our hopes and dreams. The emotions are universal, as are the ideas of looking both inward for strength and of calling out to God for help.

At the same time, particular theology does influence the content and context of prayer. It also influences the use of language in general and, in my prayers, the use of Hebrew. For example, the prayer "On the Birth of a Child" asks for God's help and support to find the "humility, compassion and wisdom to teach her/him Torah and mitzvot." In other words, parents are asking for the ability to teach God's word and God's will. This is a universal desire of all people of faith. The request, however, is made with uniquely Jewish language.

Several of my prayers end with a *chatima*, a closing line that summarizes the theme or intention of the prayer. This is a Jewish prayer formula that marks the end of a *bracha*, a blessing, with what can be thought of as a seal, much like the seal that is made on paper by a signet ring. I have borrowed some of the *chatimot* from standard Jewish prayers and have written others myself.

Q. Does that mean that these prayers are for use only by Jews?

I'm amazed by the number of non-Jews, particularly Christians and Catholics, who use my prayers. I receive frequent requests from rabbis, priests and ministers for permission to reprint my prayers and to use them in communal worship. My prayer blog is visited by people of all faiths.

A modern Jewish voice of prayer appears to appeal to Jews as well as to non-Jews. I have been encouraged by the number of non-Jews who look to my work to find a Jewish connection. Hebrew appears in about 40 percent of my prayers. So there are many pieces that are accessible to those who are uncomfortable with the Hebrew. At the same time, many non-Jews say that they appreciate the use of Hebrew and Jewish prayer styles, such as the *chatima*. The influence of Hebrew poetic forms on a modern sense of prayer creates a voice of prayer that feels both ancient and new. It seems that people are craving that connection in prayer.

Q. Classic prayer isn't necessarily comfortable or familiar to everyone on a spiritual path. What about people who describe themselves as spiritual but not religious? What do you have to offer those who shy away from any particular religious affiliation?

The lion's share of my work is written with a universal voice. I make a very conscious effort to match the voice and the language of prayer to the intention of prayer. In my work, I use many different voices, which I have named. For example, I often use the voice of "the Liturgist" when I am writing a prayer tied to a particular Jewish event or festival. For me, this is a classic Jewish voice. I also use the voice of "the Prophet." This is a universal religious voice that might also be thought of as the voice of personal challenge. This voice is typically punctuated by the call to rise up in service to God and humanity. I call one of my favorite voices "the Spiritual Traveler." This is a universal spiritual voice. It's the voice of the individual on a spiritual path, the voice of spiritual struggle and spiritual learning. When I am writing prayers for men, I use the voice of "the Awakened Man," a universal male voice of personal challenge and self-realization. Most of my prayers speak to those who identify themselves as religious and those who identify themselves as spiritual.

Q. Although you've been a writer all your life—a journalist, an essayist and a nonfiction book author several times over—you only recently started writing prayers. What happened to change the focus of your writing?

Poetry was the first stop on my journey as a writer, followed by short fiction. I began writing poetry in middle school but was highly self-critical of my work and soon lost my enthusiasm. I shifted to short stories. During my freshman year in college, I began to write for the school newspaper and found my voice writing commentaries and breaking news. Throughout college, I took freelance jobs—we were called "stringers"—for any paper that would give me work. I also took unpaid newspaper internships and earned a master's degree in governmental journalism. My first full-time journalism job was in Illinois with the *Decatur Herald & Review*. Later, I became one of the top editors for the Journals of the American Hospital Association. I had regular columns in two magazines. Occasionally, my Jewish short fiction was published in the Jewish and secular press.

In my early fifties, I began a regular practice of morning prayer, meditation and writing. The practice evolved, taking on a particular rhythm and order. I'd read from an inspirational reader, followed by a period of meditation and then a period of prayer. Then I'd write. In time, my writing took on a structure and pattern: I would write observations about myself, a gratitude list, a personal affirmation and a statement of my life mission. I would also put down two intentions for the day and then make a quick assessment of how I did with yesterday's intentions.

After about two years of that practice, some days it seemed natural to continue writing. What emerged are what I call prayer-poems: poems with elements of prayer. About a month before my wife, Ami, *z"l*, died, I became aware that my meditation and writing practice had evolved. It had become quite rich. I produced many of these prayer-poems. After she died, my connection to meditation and prayer seemed shattered, but soon I found that I needed words to pray on behalf of my daughters. I wrote a piece called "For Bereaved Children." Until that point, my prayer writing was the result of my spiritual practice. With this prayer, my spiritual practice centered on writing prayers, meditations, poetry and song. Although the core actions did not change, my intention shifted. I became a poet and a liturgist. My writing path had come full circle.

Q. Are you comfortable with the term "liturgist"?

It took me a long while to get used to calling myself a liturgist. I did not think of it myself. I first heard it when a rabbi introduced me to another rabbi as "an amazing poet and liturgist." It was rather shocking to hear the term. I always thought of liturgists as ancient mystical figures who employed a unique channel of communication to God to receive holy and secret words of prayer and blessing that could then be used by the people in worship. Liturgists were old, wrinkled and pale and were highly educated and lived on a high spiritual plane. "Liturgist," I thought. "Me? Hmm. That's interesting." Today I think of myself as a poet, a songwriter, a meditation writer and a modern-day liturgist.

Q. What does it mean to be a modern-day liturgist?

A modern-day liturgist is a witness to the essential longing that occurs in all of us during the most uplifting and the most devastating moments in our lives. A modern-day liturgist is a witness to the yearning to express our joys—and our fears—to a God, to a higher power, to the soul of the universe. Being a liturgist requires a certain kind of fearlessness, a willingness to put down on paper and into prayer the most secret and intimate truths of our lives, to capture the essential longing in all of us that occurs during the most uplifting and the most devastating moments that we face. Today's liturgist blends modern and ancient metaphors with the deepest desires of our hearts.

Q. You write about a wide range of topics, including topics that are out of the realm of your own personal experience, such as prayers for beginning fertility treatment, entering hospice care or the death of a child. Are you comfortable writing prayers outside your scope of experience? What qualifies you to write prayers outside your experience?

I wrestle with these questions regularly. Can I capture the emotions or experiences of others in an authentic voice, in a voice that resonates, in a voice that sounds genuine and true? This wasn't a particular concern at first, since I was writing only for myself. Once I began to share my prayers publicly on my website, I became much more aware of both the scope of the emotion and the theological content of my writing. Still, I stayed very close to my life experiences and personal relationship with God. Then other people began to ask me to address prayer topics that are important to them—topics outside my direct scope of experience, ranging from creating a liturgy for the anniversary of 9/11 to addressing women's health and infertility. I thought: "Who am I to write a liturgy for 9/11? I wasn't anywhere near the events and did not suffer a direct personal loss." I thought the same type of thing initially when asked to write fertility prayers. "I'm not a woman, so how can I be qualified?" And yet, others who have read my work were asking me to fulfill a need. Others were looking to me for help finding a voice for their prayers.

Q. How do you reconcile these conflicting pressures?

It depends on the situation. With the liturgy for 9/11, I jumped into the project with the explicit idea that I would write the prayers, test them with people I know with more direct experiences of the events, and scrap them if I wasn't completely sure that they would be of value and use to others. These prayers are the most read pieces of my work on my website. With the fertility prayers, I simply waited for an inspiration. The idea was suggested to me, but no one initially had expressed a direct personal need. And there are other lovely offerings available online. So I didn't feel a particular urgency to push past my own comfort zone.

Many of the common emotions and experiences that we all face at some point in our lives provide enough of a basis of empathy and connection to allow me as a writer and liturgist a sound basis for evoking an accurate tone—or, at the very least, a useful tone—in many circumstances. I also speak with people who have had direct experiences with a particular issue, such as the death of a child or a miscarriage. From time to time, I consult with writers, rabbis and other theologians, and I ask them for comments on early drafts.

Q. What was the catalyst for your fertility prayers?

I had been asked to address this topic many times but did not consider myself qualified to find the proper voice for this desire, this hope, this yearning. Yet again, a friend suggested that I write a fertility prayer, and again I gave my standard answer: How can I possibly hope to find the correct balance of petition and emotion? Two days later, I wrote this line on a scrap of paper: "Bless my body with the wonders of pregnancy and my days with the promise of birth." I set it aside to work with later.

Later came pretty quickly. Not an hour after I wrote those lines, I got an e-mail message from a friend, a Jewish educator, who had a friend with an immediate need for a prayer for a successful fertility treatment. She asked if I had something she could share with her friend. The appointment was scheduled for the next day. Could it be a mere coincidence that I wrote a line for a fertility prayer and then got a call with what amounted to a deadline? As soon as my ear and my voice opened to the topic, the call to write came. Less than an hour later, I sent my friend a draft prayer, "For Pregnancy," for her comment. My friend said that she would share it as written. Her friend relayed back that it was exactly what she needed. The next day I wrote seven more prayers on the topic, addressing issues of fertility, fertility treatment, high-risk pregnancy and loss of pregnancy.

Q. Why write prayers at all? Can't we all pray in our own voices and in our own words?

The act of writing a prayer is, in every sense, an act of prayer itself. So the first answer is that I write prayers as part of my spiritual practice of prayer. I am praying with my own words. And yes, it's true: not only can we pray in our own words, I believe that God wants to hear us pray from our own hearts. So I would rephrase the question like this: What relevance do these prayers have to others?

During their most difficult moments, some people struggle to find words to express their feelings and their needs. One aspect of relevance is providing people with language that resonates for them when they cannot find their own words. Another aspect of relevance comes from the very breadth of this book. Many topics have not yet been adequately addressed by written prayers. Still another aspect of relevance is giving permission, by example, to pray in our own words. It would be great if some people thought, "If he can write prayers, why can't I?"

GLOSSARY OF
HEBREW TERMS

Adonai: the Jewish pronunciation of the tetragrammaton, the four-letter name of God, this is a substitute pronunciation, as the actual pronunciation has been lost; lit., "the Lord"

Aliyah: to immigrate to Israel; to be called to say a blessing in front of the Torah; lit., "going up"

B'nei mitzvot: lit., "children of the commandments"; the plural of bar mitzvah, the time when a Jewish male comes of age, typically including an aliyah to the Torah; the plural form includes both boys and girls, which is how it is used in this volume

Bracha **(pl.,** *brachot***)**: blessing; benediction

Chatima **(pl.,** *chatimot***)**: the final summarizing line of a *bracha*; in classic Jewish prayer, the *chatima* always begins "*Baruch atah Adonai . . .*" ("Blessed are You, *Adonai . . .*")

Chuppah: Jewish marriage canopy

Davening: praying; from the Yiddish word *davnen*, "to pray"

Eloheinu: God; lit., "our God"

Hallelujah: a term from Psalms used to express praise for God; lit., "Praise ye the Lord"

Kavanah **(pl.,** *kavanot***)**: the mind-set of heartfelt intention in prayer; lit., "intention"

Mitzvah (pl., mitzvot): a commandment from God; a religious precept or sacred instruction; colloquially used to mean a good deed

Nefesh: soul; the Godly force that is in all things, including inanimate objects; the aspect of the soul that is related to natural instinct; lit., "living being"; instincts of the soul; one of several Jewish words for soul whose precise meaning is allusive and depends on usage and context

Neshama: soul; the aspect of the soul that contains the Divine spark, intellect and awareness of God, giving human beings the ability to strive for spiritual growth; lit., "breath"; intellect of the soul; one of several Jewish words for soul whose precise meaning is allusive and depends on usage and context

R'fu'at hanefesh: healing the soul

Ruach: soul; the life-giving force that animates all living things; the aspect of the soul that is related to emotion and morality; lit., "wind"; emotions of the soul; one of several Jewish words for soul whose precise meaning is allusive and depends on usage and context

Shabbat: the Jewish Sabbath, beginning at sundown on Friday and ending after the appearance of three medium-size stars in the night sky

Shabbat Hagadol: the Shabbat immediately preceding Pesach, the Jewish holiday of Passover, the spring festival commemorating the Jews' exodus from Egypt

Shiva: the seven-day period of mourning following interment

Shoah: the Holocaust, referring to the destruction of 6 million European Jews in 1938–45; lit., "consumed by fire"

Shofar: ram's horn, blown for religious purposes

Tanach: the Hebrew Bible

Tefilot: prayers; plural of *tefilah*

Tikun olam: repairing the world

Torah: the Law given to Moses on Mount Sinai; lit., "teaching"; the word "Torah" can be used either to identify the Five Books of Moses or as a more general term encompassing all of the Jewish Bible and holy texts

Vidui: confession recited annually on Yom Kippur, the Jewish Day of Atonement; confession recited on a deathbed

Yizkor: the name of the main prayer said during the memorial service commemorating relatives who have died; the commonly used name for the memorial service itself

z"l: abbreviation for *zichrono livracha* or *zichrona livracha*; lit., "may his/her memory be a blessing," added when mentioning in writing the name of someone who has died

ALSO BY ALDEN SOLOVY

Prayers for Healing the World—These new prayers and meditations expand the scope of *Jewish Prayers of Hope and Healing* to include prayers for healing the world. Along with new prayers for healing, the topics range from elections to revolution, from social justice to social responsibility.

Prayers from the Heart of Darkness—What do we say to God in our moments of deepest darkness? What words can express our fears and longings? This volume of new prayers addresses moments of fear and moments of loss, tackling difficult topics with sensitivity and grace.

Prayers for the Joys of Life—We are blessed with so many moments of joy and hope, laughter and celebration. This book of new prayers and meditations focuses on the formal and informal moments of wonder and thanksgiving that are part of our daily lives.

Bending Light: The Jewish Prayers of Hope and Healing Workbook—This workbook is designed to help people begin and deepen the art of writing as a spiritual practice, including essays, letters to God, prayers and meditations.

The Song of the Spiritual Traveler—This journey of the soul is a duet between two voices. The first is a narrator who weaves the tale. The second is the voice of the Spiritual Traveler, who shares the meditations that have been revealed to him on his mythic journey within.

49 Days Bending Light: Meditations for Counting the Omer—A mystical and engaging guide to the 49 days of Counting the Omer, based on *Jewish Prayers of Hope and Healing* and *The Song of the Spiritual Traveler*.

Alden Solovy is a Jewish poet and liturgist, a writing coach and an award-winning essayist and journalist. He has written for daily, weekly and monthly newspapers, as well as magazines and blogs. His short fiction has been published in the Jewish and secular press. Alden's poetic and liturgical writing was transformed in 2009 by the sudden death of his wife from catastrophic brain injury. As a result, he began to explore writing liturgy, poetry and prayer as a spiritual practice. He has written more than 400 pieces of new liturgy, offering a fresh new voice of prayer. He is available to teach, read his work and serve as a writing coach or as a liturgist-in-residence. He also leads prayer-writing classes for adults and teens and writes commissioned liturgy for congregational use. In May 2012, Alden made aliyah to Israel, where he hikes and camps whenever possible. He splits his time between Chicago and Jerusalem.